with

PEN

in

HAND

with PEN *in* HAND

writings from the
howe memoir workshop

2012-2019

Albany Public Library

www.albanypubliclibrary.org

With Pen In Hand
Copyright © 2019 by The Howe Library

Cover photo by Shannon Palmo
Book design by Jessika Hazelton

Printed in the United States of America
The Troy Book Makers • Troy, New York •
thetroybookmakers.com

To order additional copies of this title,
contact your favorite local bookstore
or visit www.shoptbmbooks.com

ISBN: 978-1-61468-528-9

Introduction

This will be a brief introduction, so you can get to the reason you're holding this book: the work of 40 writers who have something compelling to say!

In November of 2012, I offered a four-week workshop in memoir writing at Albany's Howe Library, thanks to the encouragement and assistance of Howe librarian Jim Davies. I have just found an email to Jim dated December 7, 2012, asking for a two-week extension to the course because the class was having a good time. And now, nearly seven years later, we continue to have a good time.

The membership of the workshop has changed, of course (indeed, some of these entries are from folks who have moved on but are rightly included in this volume), but the reason anyone shows up each Monday remains the same: a desire to tell her/his life story to a group of writers who will listen, be amused or moved or dumbstruck, and provide gentle feedback in a supportive environment.

Nearly all of the pieces here come from the workshop, often from prompts that I give weekly to stimulate thinking and creativity. It is such a privilege to hear new work every Monday as serious writers continue to develop their voices.

Our thanks to Shannon Palmo for her cover design and to the numerous leaders and staff at Howe over the years who have set up the room, provided various supplies, helped the class members make copies of their work, and allowed us to give public readings. In particular a shout-out to librarian Dan Barker, and enormous gratitude to Tor Loney, Howe's head librarian, for pushing us to compile this book and finding the funds to have it printed.

Thanks to the class's hard-working editorial board, who chose these pieces: Dijonnaye Daniels, Faith Green, Bob Knightly, June Kosier, Betsey Kuzia, Kathy McCabe, Jose Morales, Mary Kate Owens, and Sharon Stenson.

Finally, thanks to Jessika Hazelton and the folks at The Troy Book Makers for guiding us through the publishing process and producing the handsome volume in your hands.

Paul Lamar

Contents

A Lesson from Bambi

Judy Spevack

I was dressed up to go to the movies. I wore a dress that my grandmother had made for me for special occasions, and black patent leather shoes. The new Walt Disney movie called *Bambi* had just opened at the Paramount Theater in downtown Oakland. It was the first time that I can remember going to the movies with my father. I was very excited. The year was 1942, and I was nearly six.

A year earlier, the Japanese had bombed Pearl Harbor and many thoughts were on the war and whether it would reach our shores. All I thought about that day was going to the movies with my daddy.

He took my hand, and we walked to the ticket booth. I looked up and saw lights around the movie marquee. They were bright and flashed on and off.

My father bought two tickets and as we walked into the lobby, I looked around and saw soft red velvet chairs and couches and a stairway leading to a second level. I wanted to sit in the chairs to see how they felt, but it was time to go into the theater. We reached the door and were greeted by a pretty lady dressed in a uniform of shiny trousers that billowed out at her ankles, and a matching form-fitting jacket fastened by five bright brass buttons. She wore a small round hat that perched on her head.

In one hand, she carried a large flashlight.

"Right this way please," she said as she guided us into the theater and up a few steps to the Loge seats; you could see the movie screen better up there. "Right there, Honey," she said to me, and shined the flashlight onto one of two empty seats.

I sat down. My father sat down in the seat next to me, juggling a bag of popcorn for us to share. I looked around and saw that there were other children in the theater as the lights began to dim.

"Why is it dark, Daddy?" I asked.

"Shh. The movie is about to start."

All of a sudden the screen was full of color and light as the story of Bambi began to unfold. I wasn't sure what to expect, since I had never been to a movie before, but the animated animals moving across the screen fascinated me. I remember one part in particular, where Bambi meets his first friend.

He followed his mother into the meadow, and the first thing he saw was Thumper, the rabbit, perched on a log.

Thumper pointed to Bambi and giggled.

"He's all wobbly," he said.

"If you can't say anything nice, don't say nothin' at all," Thumper's father scolded.

I liked the friendships of the animals in the forest. When Bambi's new friend Thumper sat on a log and rapidly pounded his hind foot, and said, "Hello," then laughed and pointed at the butterfly on Bambi's tail, I laughed, too. When Bambi mistook a skunk for a flower, I was drawn into the story. When the Great Prince of the Forest appeared, I learned that he was Bambi's father. I took everything in.

The movie was not all rosy. The gunshot, the disappearance of "Bambi's mother, the fire, and the word spoken by one character—"Man"—scared me. The scenes of frightened animals running, the sky filled with birds taking flight, scary ferocious dogs with teeth bared, drool falling from their mouths—all left an indelible impression on me, as did the earlier scene when Bambi is briefly separated from his mother. It was the scene with Bambi's mother running, the sound of gunshot and Bambi calling, "Mother? Mother?" and then the arrival of Bambi's father to guide him to safety, that is seared into my memory.

The rest of the movie with Bambi's friends pairing up—Bambi with Faline, Thumper and Flower finding mates, and twittering birds flying off in pairs—softened the earlier harsh and more frightening parts. The Walt Disney movie that my father thought I would enjoy turned out to be more memorable than anyone could have imagined, particularly for me.

My dad and I walked out of the theater, hand in hand, got into the 1936 Chevy Coupe and drove home. I enjoyed spending that day with him.

I still wonder if that was the day he told me that my mother wasn't coming back. The movie certainly gave him an opportunity. She had died unexpectedly after a brief illness nearly two years earlier, but I don't remember him ever giving me a clear answer when I asked. After her death, our lives began to settle when my grandparents moved from their family home in Rockford, Illinois, to the house on 79th Avenue to care for me.

He told me years later that whenever he tried to answer my question his eyes would fill with tears and he couldn't find the courage to tell me. Someone told me that my mother was a guardian angel watching over me from Heaven. I hope he was the one who eventually took that step.

I think it was the *Bambi* movie that taught me that life continues on, even in the face of hardships. Bambi and the forest animals helped to ease me into a childlike truth. If that was my father's intention, it worked. I accepted that if Bambi's mother wasn't coming back and his father looked after him, I could feel safe with my father looking after me, even with a war going on.

Judy Spevack   (1936 - 2018)

It's Cold in Here, Irene

Kate Gleason

It sure is cold in here. This Old Navy cap should do the trick. Irene, the seller, told me, the potential buyer, that her singlewide mobile home, in Selkirk, within earshot of the fabled train yards, was warm.

In early September, under the quiet breeze of a ceiling fan, we were having tea in her kitchen, at a round oak table garnished with sunflower place mats. Irene pointed to the desultory area rug and said: *I put this down when I got here thinking the floor would be cold but it wasn't. I didn't need it after all.*

I paid cash for the home and moved in at the end of October.

NOW HEAR THIS, Irene, down in Florida less than a week in your daughter's four-bedroom house, IT'S COLD IN HERE AND IT'S ONLY NOVEMBER 8TH.

But you knew that, didn't you, Irene? That's why you left before a second winter.

Ornery as I may sound, I'm not sorry I paid you my entire savings plus fifteen hundred from a friend, for this 980-square-foot ice box, this new windows–new-roof Frigidaire anchored to a slab of concrete. Because, as I sit here wearing one of the fleece-lined hoodies you graciously and KNOWINGLY left behind, I'm writing on my laptop with a view of my golden-hearted Chihuahua as he snores in a round doggie bed which, coincidentally, matches the green corduroy of the reclining sofa and armchair you also left behind. I haven't done any writing for three years, yet here I am, six days in my new home, so cold, so angry and so pleased, that I'm able to write!

You threw in a set of rustic-style living room tables—a hefty wood coffee table, where my laptop balances on two stacked books; and two end tables, with three-way lamps standing sentinel. Each table, with a pair of doors, provides deep storage, as in a cabin cruiser. Magnetic closures hold back my comforter, flannel sheets, throw blankets, and a heavy off-white knitted bedspread. Will I need all of them this week?

I'm an indecisive shopper, overwhelmed by too many choices, so I thank you, Irene, for furnishing this living room in such a way that I, a hermit with hermit crab mentality, could move in and immediately feel at home.

You created a writer's paradise, Irene, and I thank you for your creation.

Through windows you cleaned to brilliance, I receive strong sunlight at daybreak and enjoy easy views of the changing mountain sky; when a westerly front crosses the Helderbergs, I thrill to the locomotive roar of rushing winds and the pebbly assault of pelting rain.

Today, the longer I work on the couch, savoring the savoring, the warmer my body feels. Scrappy has left his toasty bed to curl up in my lap, his head cradled in my left arm. Using two fingers and the thumb of my right hand, I tap out a new story. Directly overhead another ceiling fan gently reverse-circulates warm air surging from the floor vents.

I doubt if I have ever before felt this peaceful and relaxed at home. If mobile homes, like boats, were named, I'd inscribe this one, in gold script, *Sunny Irene*.

Dreams and Shadows

Faith S. Green

Under mystical cover of darkness
Demons and dreams meet
in a clandestine night embrace
Murky shadows dispatch fear

Demons and dreams meet
to battle for supreme power
Murky shadows dispatch fear
of what we cannot see

To battle for supreme power
Stealthy ghosts carry cryptic secrets
of what we cannot see
We vanquish demons

Stealthy ghosts carry cryptic secrets
Disbursed with sunrise
We vanquish demons
Under mystical cover of darkness

Astral Proportions

Faith S. Green

The magnitude of desperation
roiling firmament ominous
Unemployment of astral proportions
little hope on the horizon

Circumpolar spectrum blurred
by outrage of parents
who can't feed their children

Children shiver in a cluster to block
Prevailing arctic winds
Build tremendous pressure.

Tears freeing on sunken cheeks
pinhead fragments of hope
Gently nudge between the tremble
of stick-like limbs and runny noses.

Stellar interference
Stars collapse

The Act of Disappearing

Faith S. Green

(The Art of Disappearing by Naomi Shahib Nye
   "When someone recognizes you in a grocery store
   nod briefly and become a cabbage.")

I'd rather be a carrot, long and slender
instead of round and plump.
Although either is ok if speaking is not required
about the weather, my health and say
'fine' how about you?
I'll wear brown and become camouflage
with the potatoes with their thousands of
eyes turned away from the aisle.
I'd rather not say, Gotta go…take care.
Just let me crawl into the bulk bin
and close my eyes.

Miraculous Year

Ken Screven

My miraculous year is actually almost a year-and-a-half.

It began in August of 2016, August 11th, to be precise..a Thursday.. Outside, the weather station said it was a blistering 95 degrees. But inside my apartment, with its dark blue walls and 19th century architecture, the forecast had become increasingly grim. That was the day my body, my organs, my world, had reached some kind of 'failure' mode. My friends knew of my crisis and had assembled in my home to urge me to call for medical help, immediately.

I had been ignoring the provocative symptoms of a diabetic crisis. I had not left the second floor Victorian, Albany apartment that I cherished, in eight long months. It was something I didn't even realize was happening, but I knew things were bad and getting worse. And on that Thursday, my friends gathered around their sick buddy and convinced me to call 9-1-1 in hopes of getting help. Within a short time a dozen paramedics were standing in my living room, admiring the furnishings but wondering how had I allowed myself to deteriorate to this level. I could not walk down the stairs, and the paramedics quickly figured out a way to carry me, cocoon like and wrapped and supported by a thick powerful rope, one step at a time down two flights and out to a waiting ambulance that had clogged busy State Street. On that sunny summer day, the blast of the heat outside was startling, and as I was moving to the ambulance on a gurney, I was conscious of people staring and wondering what had happened to me.

In just minutes, I was in the Emergency Room at St. Peter's Hospital where, in a short time, doctors informed me my blood sugar was 600 and my A1C, which measures the concentration of glucose over 3 months, was a whopping...and mortally dangerous.... 17. A normal reading is 5.7.

Over the next 8 days I was given a crash course in how to be 'a New Ken'. How to embrace a life journey that basically did NOT include sugar....or white rice..white potatoes...pasta..or white bread. The medical staff at St. Peter's saved my life. They brought me 'back'. I was sent home with instructions on how to use my insulin...and how to live the life of a 'good diabetic'. When I saw my primary physician after going home, he told me that 80% of patients who had reached that stage do not survive. He said 'someone' was looking out for me. And that I was lucky. At that point I became a new person, determined to somehow survive this.

Three months later, in an endocrinologist's office, a stunned nurse practitioner told me my A1C was now 5.6. And she wondered how I had done this so quickly. I was told it took diabetics several years to do that..if it happened at all. She was impressed..and I began to cry.

In the 16 months since I was carried out of my apartment...apparently near death...I have transformed my eating habits dramatically. No sugar, at all! My discipline even surprises me! Although I'm not perfect. My endocrinologist has been my vociferous and constant cheerleader and I feel like a different person. My fasting blood sugar in the morning is consistently 100 or less..mostly in the 80s or 90s.. My A1C has remained 5.6..or 5.8. And those are numbers for a non-diabetic. Sticking to 'the rules' consistently has also led to my being taken off insulin entirely, three months ago. When that happened, I cried again. In gratitude.

And while I am still a big guy, I have managed to lose over 100 pounds in 16 months. When I look at photos of myself now, I seem to more and more recognize a Ken from my younger years. I am 67 now, but I don't feel whatever that 'is' supposed to be. My energy, stamina and joy of life have returned in a miraculous way. I can walk distances that would have been impossible 16 months ago. It is a struggle each day, but it's a battle I plan to win.

I have re-entered the world. I have taken control of my life. I have witnessed my own miracle year.

Pond Poem

Jean Van Dyk

Red wing blackbirds skim the rippling pond
a fat bumblebee hovers close to the grass
a mourning dove coos his sad sweet song
birds chitter and trill in throaty warbles
bullfrogs galumph in chorus

red Adirondack chairs sit empty
the split hickory sprouts tiny green leaves
an ash felled by beavers lies in the brush
bleeding hearts dangle- dance in the breeze
your red tractor is silenced
no longer whirring in the field
between lilacs and cherry trees

A memory drifts by
of the robin's nest in my window box
filled with cornflower blue eggs

At times like this
my latest painting drying
in my little house
I think of you

how I once loved you
the gentle you
of the tousled brown hair
kind blue eyes, soft lips

Where did you go my blue- eyed boy
where did you go my darling
across the pond
the pine trees
stripped bare by beetles
stand like ghost sentries

"Broken Wings Mended"

Regina Indi Jones

My arms are my wings
My wings are my arms
they give me the energy
To endure daily
My Wings
They were once broken
Twice broken
Many a times broken
My Wings
They are my strength
They give me the power to excel
My wings are my dignity
Even my smile
My laughter
My wings are my courage
My wings are my joy
My love
My peace
My wisdom
When my wings were broken
I was broken
I couldn't get off the ground
Let alone walk a mile

When my wings were broken

I was lost

I couldn't reach out to my loved ones

I couldn't speak or share what was on my mind

I was lost

What did I have to do to pay the cost

I had to get on my knees

And surrender my all to THEE One who gave me
the wings to excel

Shine surpass out last and to do extremely well

Thank you, Lord, for mending my broken wings

Now my

Broken wings are mended ♥

Poem #2

Regina Indi Jones

LORD I know and believe with all my heart and
soul that it is your desire for me to walk in success
If I walk not in the counsel of the ungodly
But delight myself in Your Word
I will be like a tree planted
By the rivers of 'Living Waters'
That brings forth fruit in due season
My leaves shall not wither
And whatsoever I do shall prosper
Lord, you love me and I surely do love you
You preserve the faithful
Intensively reward your children with success be-
cause of YOUR faithfulness and love
I possess good coverage
And my ♡ is strengthened
Let me learn to measure prosperity
And success according to the standards of your
word
Instead of the standards of this world. I desire to
be very successful in your eyes dear LORD ♡

Poem #3
"TODAY"

Regina Indi Jones

It is all about doing the right thing
And what goodness joy and peace
To my soul that I can bring
It is all about keeping the focus on myself
and not depending on anyone else
It is about walking the straight and narrow path
And remembering that it's okay to laugh
It is about fulfilling my destiny
And allowing my higher power
Who I choose to call GOD to guide me
It is about keeping a positive frame of mind
And remembering when it comes to others
To be nice and kind
It is about staying clean and sober
And remembering it's not done until GOD says
    it's over
When I get out of my bed I get on my knees to
    pray
My main prayer is that thee LORD guide my way
I asked HIM to watch over my 4 Kings
(Rodriek, Garry, Elijah Hezekiah)

And to please keep them safe
And to help me along this journey
As I seek the LORD's face
I must remember to keep the focus so that I can
   see the forest for the trees
And allow my HIGHER POWER
To continue to guide me along this journey of re-
   covery today!

Upstream

Mary Perrin Scott

(The Virgin River flows through Zion National Park)

Upstream the Virgin River meanders
Weaves its way between rock and trees
Canyon walls reach down touching the water's edge

Upstream we struggle barefoot in frigid water
Slippery rocks unseen beneath, rounded by water rush
My hand upon the shoulder of a wounded warrior

Upstream reveals breathtaking view of beauty
Wounded warrior holds tight, offering his balance
Sharing his story of lost firefighter comrades on 9/11

Upstream we hear the river flow toward us
Just as we heard the towers fall that crystal-clear day
Carving a canyon of pain in our souls.

Upstream canyon walls protect the river
We protect each other on the shaky walk
His pain and sadness flow like the river

Upstream offers recovery, hope of new life
Surrounding beauty overpowers wounds, pain and
    suffering
Bringing back laughter to the river of life.

Immigrant 1861

Mary Perrin Scott

The quiet harbor ushered in
A ship from abroad
Immigrants from afar
Search for a life of hope
Freedom's soil under foot
Conscripted by blue or grey
Thrust into uniform
Depending upon harbor of entry
North or South
Rite of passage to citizenship
"Go, join the kill"
From famine on home soil
To war on freedom's soil
Hungry souls left behind
The new unknown
Violence of another kind
From good and evil, history comes
The immigrant says
"My own days without end?"
"Or will the days end
With my last breath
In another muddy field?"

Forgotten souls
Families left behind not knowing
Ghosts roam the bloody battlefields
Weave a slow, sad pattern of death

Birdsong in the trees
Echoes the whispers of those who went before

Mary Perrin Scott

Cape Breton 1950

Eileen O'dea Roach

We left Albany that August 1950, changing trains in Boston onto Maine where we spent the night in a boarding house while Dad worked out immigration problems pertaining to reentry into Canada, neither parent U.S. citizens, yet. Once resolved, we continued through New Brunswick, Truro, onto Sydney, Nova Scotia in Cape Breton.

Jean, Pat, and I shared an upper berth while Mom and Dad shared the lower berth. When Mom went to use the bathroom, Dad poked his foot outside the privacy drape so she could find him on the way back. Instead, she grabbed a stranger's foot who leapt from behind the drape, startling Mom, who mumbled an apology. We three laughed quietly from our loft.

Warmly greeted with hugs and kisses, I met Nana, aunts, uncles, and cousins for the first time. I was six. While the Clarkes surely had more than a nodding acquaintance with tragedy, they swarmed us with love. Shortly after arrival, though, I was whisked off to spend the night with a cousin at Uncle Jack's cottage, too rustic for me. Besides, Mommy's girl didn't stray far from the roost so I balked, preferring the tranquil magic of Atlantic Street where aunts lavished us with bountiful meals. Splendid bakers and cooks, they served biscuits, muffins, scones, cakes, and eggs with Canadian ham for breakfast on fine English china with lovely linen napkins. Homemade blueberry and apple pies cooled on the windowsill, the kettle whistling for tea drunk by the gallons.

Love radiated out of Nana's eyes. Mom's, too. Like royalty, waited on hand and foot, she spent hours talking with Nana, simply overjoyed with her company. Devout Catholics, everyone attended Sunday mass faithfully. Uncle John took us for a leisurely drive in the country after mass, stopping to introduce an acquaintance. During a brief conversation, the man snidely referred to Uncle John as *the dummy*. Aunt Mary grimaced at the hurtful remark she lip-read while Mom roared from the back seat, "*That ignoramus!*" Redeemed by his American sister-in-law's gutsy response, the affable Uncle John drove off smiling, unperturbed.

Splashing about in the Atlantic, my first in the ocean, waves snagged me under. Gagging on saltwater, eyes burning, knees scraping pebbles on the ocean floor, I was plucked out by my cousin Frankie, sixteen, tall, dark and handsome, who soothed my battered ego. A hero, I shadowed him around like a puppy.

Mom's sisters crocheted fine lace doilies they sent to us on birthdays and holidays. Thoughtful and kind with active, productive lives among many endearing friends in the deaf community, their friends visited frequently during our stay. Masters of lip reading and sign language, my aunts taught me rudimentary sign language such as vowels and the name of the family dog, Toby, a black cocker spaniel. They signed among themselves adeptly with one hand, but taught me with two. One conversation became heated between Aunt Mary and Uncle John. In one fell swoop, she drew five fingers to her lips, leaned to the left and swung her fingers across her plump backside. She and Mom laughed and for a moment, I was privy to the startling realization that Aunt Mary told Uncle John to kiss her butt! I blushed, hiding my smile (ashamed of the gap between two front teeth). This same affectionate Aunt Mary showered me with love, fussed over my hair, braiding and tying the ends on top of my head just like hers, an ally who consoled me with a gentle touch on my shoulders when I stood my ground, stubbornly refusing to smile (the gap) for the umpteenth group photo.

Despite my grumpy scowl, mulish posture, arms folded across my chest, the furl in Aunt Mary's brow reflected in the photo smacks of concern for me. I adored her. Caring expressions of love left an indelible mark, like the moment Uncle Jack laid eyes on Mom, picked her up and swung her in circles or when a more subtle Uncle Ned glowed as he embraced Mom. Eyes sparkling, Uncle Ned hollered for me when he entered a room, "Where's Me Duck? Where's Me Duck?" I felt special. Except for my brothers, I had not seen such abundant, open displays of affection from other men toward Mom or me. Dad seemed a trifle jealous, a good thing.

The smell of blacktop permeated the air as sisters, cousins and I strolled the neighborhood promising to write letters when we got home. In the early hours on our day of departure, we ate breakfast and said good-bye, tears brimming. Mom and I saw them eight years later, but it was the last time they saw Dad, Jean or Pat. I returned three more times to those serene people in that serene place that calmed my mind and nourished my soul.

Krystal

Joe Levy

I'd never met anyone, the way I met Krystal.

We worked together, though we were not exactly coworkers, and I only saw her occasionally. Although one might easily have forgiven an air of resentment due to underpayment (especially given her qualifications), she brought nothing but enthusiasm and delight to her job. She made no telling cultural references, and performed no extraordinary acts in my presence, but I could sense grace in her character. I somehow knew that she was one of Our People.

I had the freedom to do my job as I pleased. It pleased me to let fly carefully aimed turns of phrase that would connect with the right sort of person, and to smuggle in twists that would engage only the right sense of humor. When two others had a spat over a rude gesture, I asked, "Do you bite your thumb at her?" Krystal hid her face in a desperate effort to avoid cracking up and derailing the entire room.

"Did you get to make Krystal giggle?" my wife began to ask me, as we recounted our workdays. Most often, my gratified smile answered before I spoke.

One day, I accidentally figured out Krystal's secret. She wasn't even there at the time. I just happened to hear an associate of hers, who did not share our culture, use a word that they were otherwise unlikely to have known. The subject came up in a general way the next week, so I said, in an off-hand way, "You've just described half my friends." To everyone else, it was an instantly forgettable moment of me yet again saying something slightly weird, but she knew that I accepted her and her community.

I would have hardly imagined that two people could connect while never conversing. We communicated in hints, references, humor, and acknowledging smiles, embedded within our overlapping work. On second thought, strike that: I'm shy. "Hints and references" always seemed like a fine way of sounding out a potential friend. It's just that they had never been very effective, nor so reciprocated, until now.

My wife took the initiative to state what I knew, but hadn't said because saying it out loud would commit me to action: "We should invite Krystal to dinner."

At the end of a meeting two weeks later, we said our goodbyes and turned from each other, with a palpable tension of unspoken sentiments in the air. I felt like a high schooler trying to gather the nerve to ask someone out. Everybody filtered out of the room, leaving Krystal to finish her work. I made sure I was last to reach the door, and said, "Krystal..."

She turned to me, and her mask vanished. I glimpsed an expression of hope rescued just as it was lost. Her face spoke, as clearly as any hint we had exchanged, "Oh my gods, I think he's going to say what

I want to hear." If she had been a cat, her tail would have quivered.

One might have thought that this glimpse would answer my question and quell my nervousness, but only if one did not know me well.

"I was talking with my wife, who said that since I kept mentioning this awesome consultant I work with, I should invite you to our dinner-"

"Yes," she interrupted.

"Which we hold every couple weeks. It's a-"

"Yes."

"Pot-luck with some of our friends, and your spouse-"

"Yes."

"Is invited, of course."

"Yes," she confirmed again.

I shut up.

She told me her not-actually-a-secret. "So the surprise twist is that I'm polyamorous."

"Then your partners are invited. And I think we've established that that's not much of a twist among my friends," I reminded her.

"Yes, there was a comment to that effect," she agreed.

The pot-luck dinner was the best we'd had in years.

Ticket to Ride

Nancy Dunlop

By 1968, the Revolution had seeped into the Long Island suburbs. I was seven. One summer night, my father and I took a walk. But this wasn't just a stroll. This was reconnaissance. A generational mission to check out the times.

What we found as we rounded the corner toward the boat basin was a churning mob in the making, as stoned and privileged white teens ran around the docks, whooping war cries. They created their own momentum, ready to burst through the low fence surrounding them, challenging barriers, private property, outmoded morés.

My father watched, large and clenched. A man being robbed. We turned and walked wordlessly back to the house, the howlings of a generation too young for him to understand, too old for me to join, haunting us in the night. We went back to the house with the eagle plaque over the door, and my father turned the lock.

It was odd to be a kid as the Sixties hemorrhaged. My friends and I were young enough to miss specifics about Vietnam, the race wars, assassinations of final hopes. But we knew something was up and searched in little-kid ways for clues to the culture. I searched extra hard. To be a child of the Sixties was unsettling enough. To be one raised by Victorians caused a generational chasm. While my friends' parents came of age in the 1950s, my parents were older by a decade. My mother, too, was raised by older parents, themselves Victorians.

Where to turn? My big sister. Ten years my senior, and a bona fide teenager. Hippies circled her periphery, the counterculture evident in her yearbook, with a boy who had been to California and back, wishing her Peace and Love by his Senior picture. To me, she seemed to qualify for some kind of ticket to this new world, and I studied her—her habits, her dress, her music, her shampoo bottle, her mystery bra . . . whatever . . . trying to be like her.

My sister knew what she wanted. She wanted the Beatles. As a teenager, she could have them in a way I couldn't. But I watched as she brought LPs of the Fab Four into the house, sneaking them past the Victorians. I didn't ask her who her favorite Beatle was. But in secret, I chose mine. My favorite was George.

Soon, my sister left for college, where she found herself surrounded by protest movements, straggly, long-haired boys, dope, and the Allman Brothers. She'd come home for holidays with progressive changes in her look and tastes. Her hair went from short and perky to long and stringy. She arrived in a mini skirt one semester, a maxi coat the next, her hemlines rising and falling with the cultural roller coaster. She also brought new records home: *Jesus Christ Superstar*,

Cream's *Disraeli Gears*, *The Concert for Bangladesh*. These were shoehorned into her collection of early Beatles.

She was changing fast. Growing up and getting out. She never knew the unbridgeable chasm her leaving caused in me. She was just a girl going to college. But it signaled that she was straining against and getting away from the Victorians, leaving me alone with them. She found her ticket to ride. And she took it.

* * * * * *

Shortly before Christmas 2001, George Harrison died. On the night he died, I called my sister. She was surprised that I wanted to talk about him. She said, Yes, George had been her favorite, too, but she lost interest in the Beatles when they did *Rubber Soul*. Over 30 years had gone by, and I hadn't been paying attention. While George still lived fiercely and brightly in me, he was barely a blur in my sister's memories. And even though we had both long since moved far *away* from the Victorians, she had moved *on*, while my mind was still locked in the house with the eagle over the door. When I hung up the phone that night, I realized it was for me, alone, to find my way out.

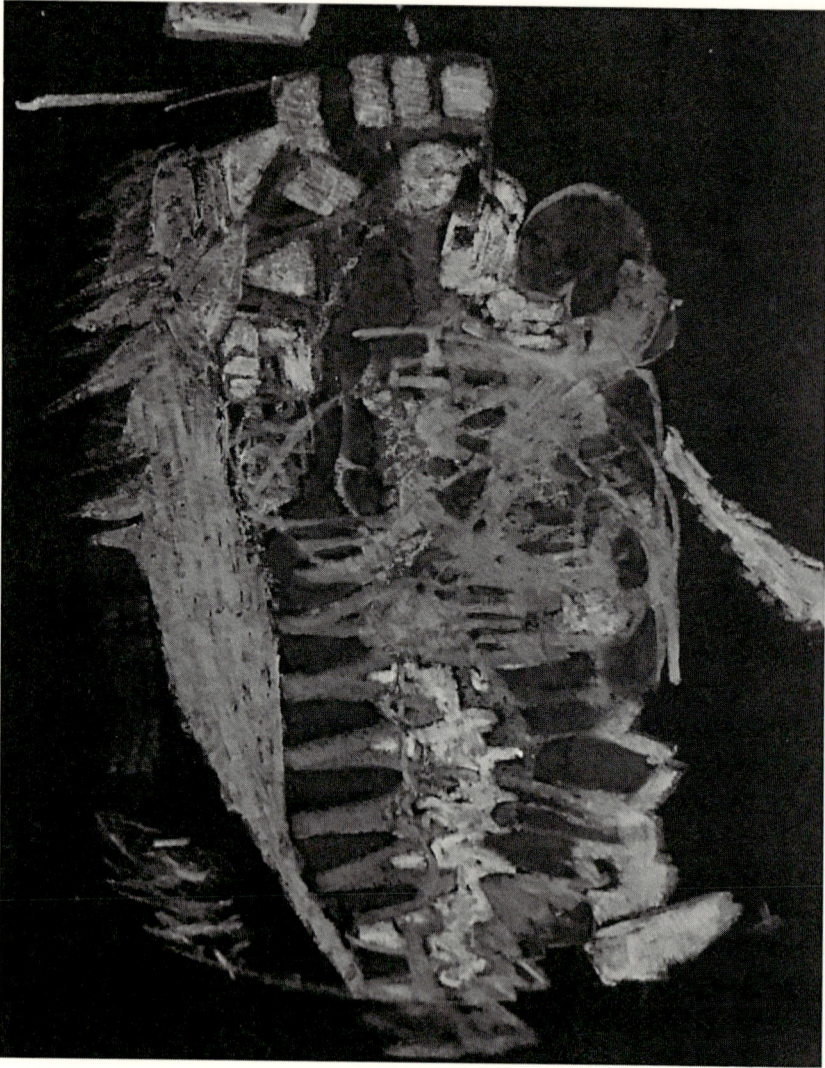

Joan Oliver

Dark Delight

Joan Oliver

Lumbering, weighed down
thin pale spotlight rays
pulse past dark depths
of serpentine routes that stray away
apparatus halts progress
familiar effort like a dead habit
no mercy that relentless process
sinks, stalled and desperate
faint hope diminishing
beneath the wingless bundle
tethered to a remote sign
encumbered with wait.
Panting hot breath illumines
cold groves of mystery
silhouettes that acquiesce
steady rhythms beat
effortful failure finishes first
a slow second ahead of tempo
tempting the circuitous path
past certain stalemates that await
justice cornered to abate
partnered with bleak forms
merciful hate beckons behind
tempting fate.

Strapped synapses
impregnated by bliss
taunt and hint at hope
weighty worthless encumbrances
willed by ancient ancestral debate
trials bears down timeless
tunnels of fake love
stalled shameless serenades
haunt directionless prompts
lead through wreckage and waste
where no souls await.
Robbed of fuel and fed up
the cruel crumbling chaos creates
blurred visions of rest and gives way
to dark delight and familiar fantasies
of fearless finds that
lurk behind the crude crust
like phantoms gifted at birth
tied down from time immemorial
a beckoning chant to pursue
imprisoned within a dank blue agate.

Deep wounds hover
a flurry of pests
hot and dry the passage
unveils burnt bundles of refuse
annihilated armor cast aside over
cliffs into cavernous depths
the blinders handed off again
generations pause and pretend
the path is plain make a mockery
of mindful meditations
affixed to crucifixions
of souls abandoned in plain sight.

Youngest of Three

Joan Oliver

Abused wife, adoptive mother, artist; bait shedder, bartender, bibliophile, bird watcher, book collector, Bruce Springsteen fan; cat napper, Catholic, collagist, collector, college graduate, concert goer, cook, creative, crow lover; Dale Carnegian, dare doer, daughter, dawn dweller, dune shacker; early riser, English major; Facebooker, fire walker, Fleetian, Floridian, Friend of Bill's; gal Friday, gallerist, geomancer, gardener; heterosexual, home owner, hostess; Instagramer; librarian, list maker; Mainer, maker, Massachusite, meditator, mender, metaphysician; native New Yorker, nature lover, neighbor, networker, niece; Palm Beacher, pet person, photographer, poet, polliwog ponder, prayer asker, problem solver, proposal writer; reader, relocator, resourceful, river walker, rope swinger; Science of Minder, sea lover, seamstress, seminarian, sentence diagramer, sister, swimmer; Taurean, traveler, triathlete, twice baptised, waitress, walker, youngest of three.

Summer Romance

Silvia Mioc

In Love (June 25)

You gave me wings to fly!
I feel like a butterfly, going from flower to flower,
    bringing joy to the world …
My heart is radiating, my eyes are shining,
I silently spread loving kindness to everyone
    around me.

Heartbreak (September 7)

I lived in the land of loneliness for a long time
You came out of nowhere and rescued me
You were my hero
Now you're gone and I'm hurting

You opened a rusted door which I can't get shut
The draft of memories is coming through - inti-
    macy, conversations, Vermont, my garden …
I need to close that door tight, move on

That is what my mind tells me, but my heart feels
    otherwise
It wants to hold on to the inebriating connection I
    still feel when I remember …

It is as if my body is possessed by the emotions
    behind memories, which grew roots in my core
If I let them go, I'm back to loneliness, scarcity
If I let them be, I'm still with you...

Why do you live so close that I have to walk
    the same streets,
        by the same restaurants,
Think it is you when I see a double-cab white
    Chevy Silverado?
How can I prevent my heart from sinking deep
    into the ground every time I pass by?
How can I rip apart my surroundings from our
    togetherness?

I go out with others, they are smitten - but I feel
    empty inside
"*Fake it until you make it*" they say, so I go through
    the motions... to no avail ...

Did I do something wrong?
Were you scared?
What happened?
"Off to Vermont to fix a leaky roof" you said –
    and then dead silence

It is hard to be alone after a flash of happiness
    with you.

I am determined to migrate to the world of love
and abundance, and never return.
Where is the one who can join me in my journey?
Are you close by?

Peace Again (October 6)

I'm on top of the mountain, looking into the
distance, seeing the splendor of the
Northeast Fall
It was an arduous climb

I lie back on a warm rock and completely
surrender to the beauty around me
I'm grounded and feel my soul opening up to the
blue sky painted with clouds
My energy is an upward river that meanders with
curiosity, and dances around those clouds
I am happy and light, close to the divine, full of
gratitude that my heartbreak is behind me
I'm free from his spell, and I'm inspired
I am one with the universe, and feel connected to
Mother Earth, who supports and nourishes me

I sit up and with my eyes gently caress the peaks in
the distance and the soft curves of the valleys
The colors – reds, yellows, oranges, and greens –
are vibrant and sparkling

It is as if the trees bloom again in the fall, reaching
their best, most majestic expression
How did they get there? Cold weather and rain…

I belong … A blissful summer, followed by the cold
of grief and the rain of tears
My soul explodes into vibrant and sparkling reds,
yellows, oranges and greens

I'm blooming with wisdom and intense contentment

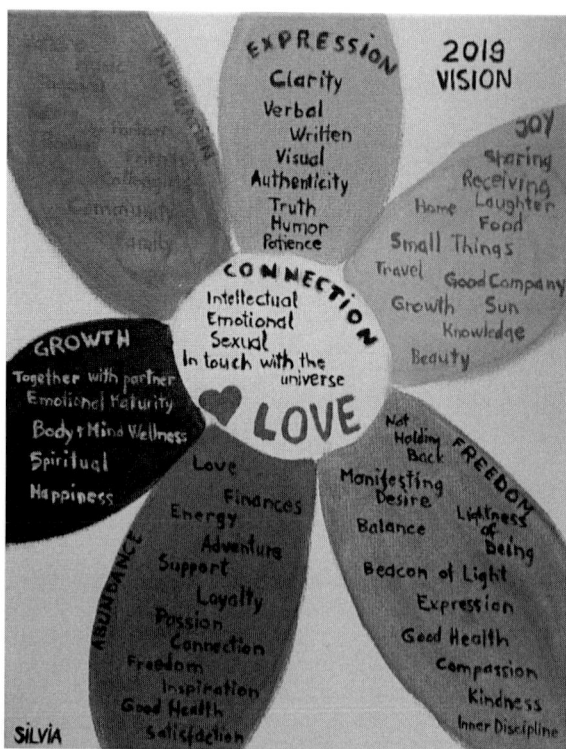

School Days: Making a Break

Robert Knightly

I ran away from home for the first time at age twelve.
I told Nan and Aunt May that I had discovered a "vo-
cation." If you went to a Catholic school, you know
what that means: you are choosing to enter a religious
order of some group—in those days, their number approached infinity, or so it seemed to a boy just entering
puberty. It also meant that I'd be leaving home: aban-
doning them is how it looked to Nan and Aunt May. I
knew that as surely as I knew I had to get away, even
if I couldn't say it or knew why I felt that way. Instead,
I said that God had told me to join the Franciscans.
That kind of declaration forestalls any inquisition, any
but the most muted expressions of alarm in an Irish
Catholic family (lukewarm in the practice as its adult
members might be)—something I instinctively knew.

The Franciscan Order of Teaching Brothers
taught all the boys' classes at St. Anthony of Padua
Grammar School after our fourth year, so it never oc-
curred to me to sign up with anyone else. I knew the
priests by sight and by name but had never spoken to
any of them outside the Confessional. They were only
a little more remote to me than my father, whom I saw
on the holidays at our house, and on those occasions
when I'd have to visit with him and one of his wives

at their house: either in the Polish section of Green-point or Astoria, Queens, or Morristown, New Jersey, depending on which wife it was. Actually, I liked the three of them, who were always kind to me. I bore them no ill will; it wasn't as if I had ever known my mother. And I came to see that living with my father, their lot was not a happy one. So, I was never in danger of becoming a priest.

I was kind of a religious kid, even a bit on the scrupulous side. Never missed Mass on Sundays and Holy Days, and tried to pay attention and commune with the statues of the saints heavily represented in our cathedral-sized church. It seemed right to me how our church was at the top of well-to-do Milton Street where it dead-ended at Manhattan Avenue, the main thoroughfare into and out of Greenpoint, Brooklyn, like an arrow shot through its heart.

Looking up Milton Street towards the church, you'd see the Priests' House on its right, the Nuns' Convent on its left. I never entered either one of those houses, just the church, like I said. I was a scrupulous kid back then, mainly when it came to examining my conscience before going to Confession, the weekly Friday afternoon ordeal. It wasn't the lying to my aunt that I hesitated to tell Fr. O'Connor (and it always seemed to be that giant, red-faced Irishman in the Box), or the disrespectful lip that I might have given her on occasion (actually, it was more in the realm of thought than deed)— it was the impure thoughts that got me. I knew I had them, all right, and plenty of them, but I could never figure out if I had crossed over that line between being "tempted" or "entertaining" them—the former being allowed while the latter was a sin, so that tallying up my list of transgressions while fidgeting on the hard-wood kneeler in a pew just outside the purple-shrouded Confessional in the darkened basement below the main altar made me break out in a sweat under my school uniform as, chance would have it, I'd lock eyes on the Station of the Cross affixed to the wall next to the Confessional, depicting Jesus sweating blood as He prays in the Garden of Gethsemane while His enemies are nearby, waiting to pounce. When it was finally my turn, I'd enter the box, kneel down facing Fr. O'Connor hiding behind the screen, and disgorge everything in my head as if I'd just eaten a bad clam, just to be on the safe side. Once, driven by fear of eternal damnation, I'd dared to ask Fr. O'Connor if I was doing it wrong and that's why I was having such trouble. It was he who told me, in his thick Galway accent, that I had this "scrupulosity," and it was a good job I was doing. When I'd finish and be excused, I'd leave the box and go to the altar rail to say my penance—twelve Hail Marys and six Our Fathers—with a spring in my step and feeling light-headed.

A RIVER OF DANCING BEARS

Robespierre

SHE WROTE ME THAT
BIG HOUSES DREW CIRCLES
IN HER MEMORIES
LIKE THE SINGING CORPSE
OF BEBOP MUSIC
PLAYED UPSTAIRS.

SHE WROTE ME THAT
THEY THOUGHT
SHE WAS HIS SISTER.
SHE SAID SHE JUST MADE IT UP
ON THE SPOT.
SHE WAS ALWAYS DOING
STUFF LIKE THAT.

SHE WROTE ME THAT
SHE TOLD THEM
SHE HAD SEEN THE LIGHT
AND THE ERROR OF
THE MAGAZINE STORIES.
BUT, NOBODY KNOWS
HOW TO READ, ANYMORE.

SHE WROTE ME THAT
SHE ARRIVED EARLY
EVERY VISITING DAY
NOT MISSING ONE
FOR THIRTEEN MONTHS
BEFORE HE SAID
WORD ONE.

SHE WROTE ME THAT
SHE DREAMED OF GOOD-HUMORED
    CANNIBALS.
BUT I SUSPECTED THESE
DREAMS HAD BEEN STOLEN
FROM EVER SEARCHING
SOMNANBULISTS WHO
HAD JUST CROSSED OVER.
THEY COULD HAVE BEEN
DREAMS THAT HAD KEPT
SILENT AND SLEPT
FOR FAR TOO LONG.
THERE WAS NO WAY OF TELLING
WHEN IT WAS THAT LATE
IN THE SEASON.
THEY COULD HAVE BEEN DREAMS
FROM THE LAST
SANDCASTLE CINEMA
AWAITING THE TIDE.

AFTER ALL
THERE HAD BEEN ONE
NOT FAR FROM
HER PART OF TOWN.

ONE AFTERNOON
AT THE BUS STOP
I THOUGHT I SAW THE LOOK
OF A BAREFOOT DREAMER
IN HER ENDLESS EYES,
WARM WET FEET DANCING
UPON COOL WET LEAVES
UPON COOL WET SIDEWALKS.

HE WROTE ME THAT
ONE WORDLESS DAY
SHE HAD ARRIVED
IN A HURRY,
RUNNING DOWN CORRIDORS,
LAUGHING AT
SILK STOCKINGS,
HOLDING HIGH
STILETTO HEELS,
ALL EXCITED
READY TO JUMP ROPE.
HE WROTE ME THAT
IN A CORNBREAD WHISPER
SHE DESCRIBED
A RIVER OF DANCING BEARS

AND THE OVERCROWDED BOATS
THAT TRIED SO HARD
TO LOSE THEIR WAY.

HE WROTE ME THAT
HE SPOKE ONLY AFTER
SHE MENTIONED
THE MUSIC.
AND NOW I BELIEVE HER.

Poems

Jose Morales

Spanish Harlem Fire

1950, when sudden knocks and loud Spanish
    shouts, "*Fuego! Fuego!*"
awaken my parents to gray smoke swirling in our
    apartment
Papi grabs my brother from bed and Mami grabs me
lights go and Mami and I fall rolling and tumbling
feeling for black steps until Mami says we need help
and we blindly find my godparents' door who
    sleepily answer
her knocks and tell her not to worry firemen
    arrived
but Mami shouts out the fire escape window for
    help
I look and see shiny red fire engine trucks below

Your Kiss

Your love is guaranteed me,
its demonstration alive
in the ardor of your kiss,
soulful, as sweet as all
that delights me.

And I respond, inflamed,
with lips caressing yours,
opening in desire to sink deeply
into you, lost, but aware that my heart
is imprinting a delicate memory,

Prayer of a Bullied Child

His tears have been suppressed,
outwardly he puts on a brave face,
it's as if he has been quarantined,
he stands alone in the outside world
and worse, alone within himself.

Taunts and ridicules echo loudly,
repeating themselves in his head,
perhaps pounding his pillow will help,
perhaps an angry unrestrained scream
will put a brake on his ache and pain.

Tonight he fretfully prays again :
"Our Father...*where art Thou?*
Hallowed be...*please, please, I am blessing Your name.*
Thy kingdom come...*take me where I will be safe.*
Thy will be done...*please take away the pain!*
On earth...*help me right here, right now.*
Give us this day...*each day I pray for just one friend.*

And forgive...*me, and my ugly, ugly faults.*
As we forgive those...*how do I forgive?*
And lead...*me not to hate or hurt myself.*
But deliver...*me from this hell...*
Amen...

La Chancleta...The House Slipper

At a table during a visit
with my cousins in Phoenix
we recall, how long ago,
our mothers chased us
with a chancleta in hand...
"Mami, no!, No, Mami!"
*<< **Pow!** >>*

Our mamitas tolerated
no battle of wills
at a dinner table,
nor muttering
during a scolding,
or we'd see
them armed
with the mighty
Puerto Rican
child-taming,
mother-weapon
of discipline:

the ever-ready,
ever under-foot,
handy-to-grab,
slip-off chancleta…
<< ***Pow!*** >>

Chancletas are now artifacts
of humor, filling our eyes
with honey tears,
blending with
Latino-patented guffaws,
as we offer ever-more-elaborated
chancleta episodes.

Three Barns Later

Stephen J. Roberts

It was around 2007 or 2008 when I started horseback riding. Since then, I've been at three different horse stables. I started at JHA (Just Horsing Around) Riding Academy. Then it was on to Placid Hills for about a year-and-a-half. The last six years, I have been at New Horizon Stables.

As a horse lover and a horseback rider, I learned to mount the horses and how to clean them with three different brushes and combs. The three different brushes and combs are a curry comb, a soft brush, and the dandy brush, which is coarse. It depends on how dirty the horses are. Then we use a hoof pick to clean around the tender part of the horse's hoof, which is called the frog, looking to their back right from the right back leg and then to the left side while the horses are on crossties to keep them in place.

There are many different breeds of horses. I ride a horse named Tiz. My friend Jim rides a pony named Crystal. Tiz is a thoroughbred and Crystal is a Welsh pony. Tiz is a sorrel-colored horse with a white strip running down the middle of her head. As for Crystal, she is a cream-colored horse. Then you get a horse named Hans, who is a Chestnut horse and then I move on to Polly, who is a black horse. There are two other guys in the Wednesday afternoon group who ride horses with us. One of them rides Polly and the other one rides Hans. In the end, it is a total of five guys who go horseback riding. One more thing to remember is to have your hand out straight when you give a horse an apple or a mini candy or even a carrot. Why, you say? The horse may bite you. As for our horse instructor, Laurie, she owns a horse named Lulu. She lets one of the other guys walk her horse Lulu around the arena. She is fun to have around us and she is funny.

After that, we get everything to get ready to go riding. It goes like this: The first thing is the saddle pad and then the wither pad and then the English saddle or a Western saddle. The Western saddle is heavier and has a horn on the front, which can make it easier for a newcomer. It will depend on which one you are comfortable with. Then the girth and last the reins. When it comes to the reins, sometimes we get help with them, if the horse is agitated or excited. Then the reins go over the horse's head, and the halter with the mouth bit goes in the horse's mouth. You should always walk around to the front of the horse.

Over the last year or so, I have been saying it's more like a relaxation class than a horseback lesson for me. Three of the horses I remember I rode when we were at JHA Riding Academy were Demo and a horse named Gus and my boy Trouble. At the Placid Hills Stables, I rode a horse named Leo.

Now we come to where I am today at New Horizon Stables. Here I have been on horses named Ben, Lyric, Crystal, Polly, and Hans. At times, it may be a horse named Montana. Then you know my girl Tiz. My friend and I have played games like Dizzy Izzy (where we ride to one end of the barn, dismount, spin around and try to run back) and Alligator Pole (where we try to ride our horses through two poles that get closer and closer together). I even did some cantering at the last two places, but nine times out of ten, my friend and I do trotting.

My all-time favorite horse that I rode was my girl Tiz. I've ridden in the Special Olympics three times. The first one was October the 8th of 2016 at the 4H Learning Center. The second was on October the 2nd of 2017. In 2018, it was at New Horizon Stables. In all the shows, I rode twice on Hans and twice with my princess, Raven.

When we are done riding the horses, we bring them back in the other barn to untack the horses. We take off the reins, put on the halter, and we put them back on the crossties. Then we take everything else off of the horses. Next, we put their blankets on them and then we use a lead rope to walk them back out to their paddock, or sometimes to their stalls. We leave the halter with them and bring the lead rope back with us. Then we say, "Good bye. See you next week!"

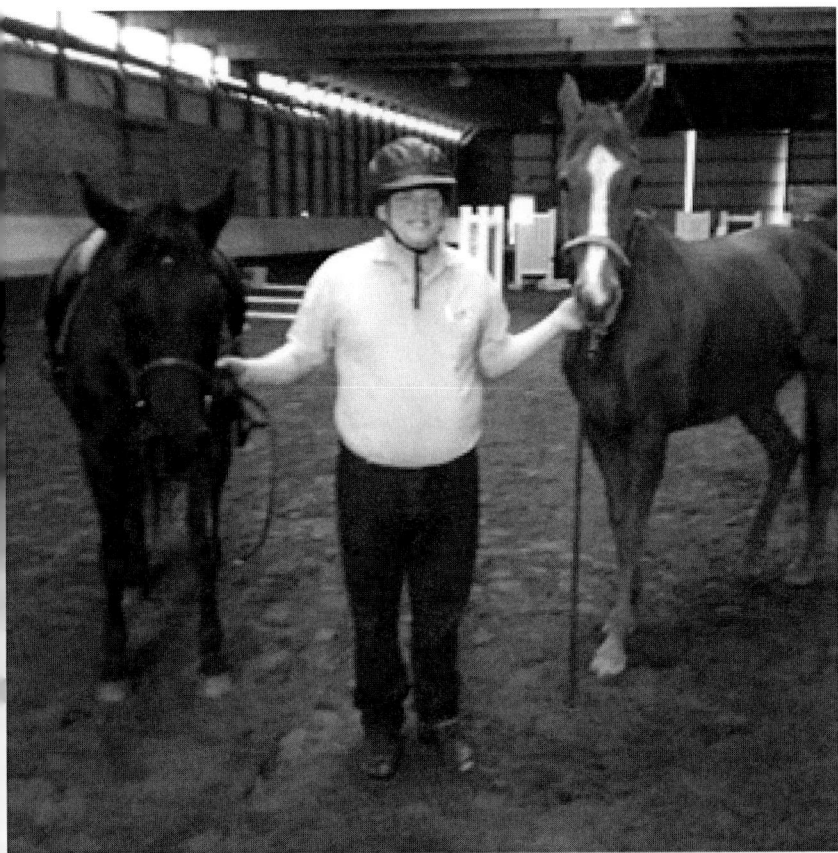

elegy

Sharon Stenson

dear dead tavern on a tear-slicked city street
there, among the empty eyes and bottles of hope
we fell in love with love

dear dead marriage that carried me to the day
when the idea of you crumbled

dear teen Romeo and Juliet
I see you still as you dance that
slow slow dance
on the oiled wooden floor.

dear dead Elvis who sang for us
from the juke box that night
"It's down at the end of Lonely Street
at Heartbreak Hotel

"It's so lonely, baby.
It's so lonely.
It's so lonely, I could die."

tango de muerte

Sharon Stenson

the lover is dancing away over the rooftops
of Bogota quicksilver feet stealing the glittering
Colombian nightsky he is doing a slow dance
tango de muerte with each improbable step
the poppies bloom Whump! now the left shoulder
he brings his arm across his chest to protect himself
Whap! the right side of the neck Thunck!
the upper thigh where last night she could have
touched him if only she could have touched him
and now the pocket of the iridescent white shirt
red petals spreading
in dreams they run through the sand
to the edge of the sea she is saying
I wanted to tell you that I loved you
but I was afraid

Villanelle

Sharon Stenson

We are always learning to leave
from the time we are born into this life.
We bear the burden and so we grieve.

We tell the stories we love to weave.
They're filled with happiness or strife.
We are always learning to leave.

The child who loves the world believes
it will always be bathed in light.
We bear the burden and so we grieve.

The adult who goes from home cannot conceive
of how he's lost his way. His life is rife
with tears. We are always learning to leave.

In old age we are not deceived
that the childhood self is gone forever.
We bear the burden and learn to grieve.

And still the moment when we receive
our fate is like a prayer
We are always learning to leave
We bear the burden and learn to grieve.

Planet Fitness

Paul Lamar

I have joined a gym.

Again.

When the first blast of cold weather came our way last month, I suddenly did not feel like throwing on my running clothes and trotting over the Corning Bike Trail, as is my custom.

Instead, I went to the East Greenbush Planet Fitness, whose motto is: No Gym-Timidation. OK! I thought. But on second thought, to a 69-year-old—well, not so much. One look around the room at the multifarious forms of youthful protoplasm puts paid to that come-on.

I dragged my bag of bones to the desk, where a bright-eyed young woman talked me through the sign-up, took my dough, and pointed me towards the locker room. Note to self: do not bring your gym clothes in a Price Chopper plastic bag.

The locker room was familiar: the sounds of locker doors banging, shower water hitting the tiles, towels snapping. No, actually there were no snapping towels: I just had a flashback to 1958 at School #16. I picked locker 45, which I thought was clever, because that was the year I was born. However, there were no guarantees that locker 45 would always be free, so next time I might have to come up with another number and another mnemonic device to remember where I'd left the Price Chopper-er, Market 32 bag.

I was quite lucky, however, when it came to the combination of the lock I had just purchased . It's 20-25-30. But, of course, now that I've told you, I'll have to get another lock.

I left the locker room and headed for the treadmill. This was not going to be difficult. Being a runner, I knew I could establish a comfortable pace and maintain it. Indeed, I quickly got into a rhythm and began surveying the scene.

For the next half hour I mulled over a few questions: If I were to roll off the machine and hurt myself, would I be allowed back? Is it truly possible for a human being to have calves that thick, and how did she get them? Have I really been running only 11 minutes? Do I have enough gin for two martinis? What is up with all these tattoos? And, finally, if I decide to get one, where should I put it?

After the half hour was up, I strolled over to the weights. I picked up a couple of 25-pound weights, put them right back where they belonged, and retrieved two 15-pound weights. I sat on a bench and began curling, looking straight ahead into the mirror and wondering how long it would take me to look like the guy on the next bench over. Probably nine years. In nine years I'll be 78, but I'll be a fit

78, maybe up to those 25-pound weights with no problem. I might even be able to get a senior- senior discount. I wonder if we'll have a 60th Albany High Reunion. No doubt I'll still be on the committee. I wonder if any of those boys from the School 16 locker room will be there.

After the bicep curls I decided to try some bench presses for my chest, a neglected body part. These days I am so preoccupied with keeping my pillbox organized and trimming ear hair that I have little time for pecs. I lay down on the bench and began hoisting the bar, sending shock waves through my left shoulder. Then I recalled an injury I had incurred last year when I opened the car window at 65 miles per hour to shake my fist at a truck driver who was, by my lights, doing something highly inappropriate on the highway. What happens when you put your arm out at 65 miles per hour is a law of physics, I think—something about every action having an opposite and equal reaction, maybe? But I took Latin IV instead of physics. I put the barbell down and returned to the locker room.

30-20-25. That was the combination, yes? No. 20-30-25. I monkeyed with the lock until it popped open. I stuffed the gear into the Price Chopper bag, gave my bald head a good wipe with the hand towel, and, carrying the bag in my right hand, made for the door. The young woman who had signed me up raised her eyebrows as I passed by the desk.

"Everything OK? Will we be seeing you again?"

"But, of course," I replied. "It was a grand experience. I'm going to tell my father about it and see if he'll sign up, too."

Her eyes widened.

"Take care, and I'll see you on Wednesday."

Sweet Goodbyes

Dijonnaye Daniels

At first it is filled
with soft hellos
cool and tranquil like swift tides
a heart is alive

it knows of no bitterness
no quarrels with sharp eyes
like a bird that flies
reigning high above the sky
it is effervescent
it is the sun amid its rise

then the storm comes
where the harshest symphony
resides, rage is realized
sorrow swells
heavy tears spill from the eyes

and in an instant
a spirit is silenced
to bear the agony of simple hellos
knowing sweet and painful goodbyes
will come.

House of Lilies

Dijonnaye Daniels

The sun has fallen from its bough;
 it shall be dying soon.
And I with my palms outstretched
 will have gone with the moon.
Oh, *young one*, be kind to the crust of time.
It is a gift and there is no fortress greater;
Mark not your days with spite, do not cast weight
upon your chest with the songs of wrong or right
for life will have its way anyhow
 and truth will know
your name before hate falls in and down
at your feet and its scales tip your crown.
My friend, know that your smile
 is not to be sacrificed
know that it should not be sold; to pay the
expense of death's laughter foolishly on time's dime.
Do not linger in the moments past for too long;
 they will
have gained you nothing.
 We all have tales of seeds to sow.

Dream

Dijonnaye Daniels

Sitting on the margin of day
awake, as light extends beyond reach
shrinking to crumbs before my feet
a vision comes unexpectedly
sorrow stood at my door
wrapping its arms around me
burying me atop its bones
gathering in haste between my fingers
falling sterile between my lips
its crimson tide lustful and cunning
its vanity stern
masterful in stature
no more did a star glow gold
no more did a dream
have a place to rest.

Holy Punch Line

Michael O'Farrell

In the early morning hours of Thursday, October 9th, 1958, Eugenio Pacelli, better known as Pope Pius the XII, died. Since his papacy began in early 1939, Pius XII was the most eminent and prominent figure in the worldwide Roman Catholic Church in my young life at that time. To a very religious boy closing in on 10 years old, the pope was something of an elusive figure, rather devoid of personality, literally a living figure head as opposed to a real person.

With Pius's demise, or number 260 in a long line of papal lineage, to be exact, discussion of such a historical event was a given in my fourth-grade class at St. Clement School, headed by our teacher, Sister Mary Doretta. Sister wasted no time opening the discussion, since religion was our first subject of the day, and a relief in a sense as our Baltimore Catechisms never left our desks against the chance that such a catastrophe might occur.

The particulars of that discussion have long vanished in my mind's eye, but I suppose the class concentrated on the pope's illness leading up to his death. Sister Doretta was big on suffering, having in the past regaled us students with the goriest of stories of saints who were martyred in a myriad of ways. There was no doubt that sister embellished things to a great degree, so that to merely die was not good enough. Many a saint went through the tortures of the damned, not discounting that some actually did, but Sister had her own theater of pornography that made martyrdom an unforgettable aural and visual experience.

I have no idea how long this discussion went on, but a fairly good portion of the morning class was devoted to it, with students contributing their own thoughts regarding the Pope's passing. Sister probably mentioned details of the upcoming election of the new Pope, including the telltale smoke stacks that would announce said election to the faithful of the world.

Sitting in one of the back rows of the class was John Osenkowski, who, even though ensconced in his chair and desk, towered over every boy and girl in the class. Tall and gaunt, bespectacled and unkempt, John stood out, standing head and shoulders over everyone, adult staff included. John was a gentle soul. Smart, too, but he seemed to be in a permanent fog most of the time. Being a daydreamer myself, I could somewhat relate.

Eventually the discussion wound down, and just as Sister was starting to go on to the next subject, John's hand shot up. Sister may not have noticed, as I seem to recall John trying to get her attention. She looked up. "Yes, John?"

With that, John stood up. He looked taller than ever, and with what was about to happen, more vulnerable than he had ever been before.

'Sister, the Pope died."

A wave of laughter, a roar actually, filled the room. Sister tried her best to quell the noise, but it seemed to get louder with every second. Snide remarks came next, a cacophony of sarcasm and smirks that no doubt drifted through the closed classroom door and down the hall. John simply stood there, frozen, a human dart board, a Saint Sebastian unable to avoid the slings and arrows of ridicule aimed his way. Sister Doretta admonished him, not as cruelly as I thought she might, seeing that he was punished enough as it was.

Beginnings

Anne Rokeach

A country road. Little traffic. Quieting thoughts roving through my mind. Signs—"pick UR own" and "strawberries"—grab my attention and take me back in time.

There was a large field downhill from my childhood home, between us and the one-room schoolhouse where my older brother and sister learned under the watchful eyes of Mrs. Lowell. Some of my first memories were made in that field. It was so huge that to see beyond it I needed to scramble down a gully that was deeper than I was tall, cross the mud at the bottom, climb up onto the dirt road that bore our name, and look down the hill. Only then could I see the schoolhouse and imagine what Junior and Breeta were doing. As much as I wanted to be there with them, I was deliriously happy because I was *outside*!

Mum and I had gone to the field with pans and my tin bucket. It was wild strawberry season. Strawberries were plentiful that year, just two years after my birth. Mum said the strawberries were little and sweet, just like me. One little red berry, when plopped into my mouth and squeezed by my tongue, exploded into delight. A lot of those little red berries colored my fingers a delicious red and filled up my tummy. Junior and Breeta might be in school, but *I* was the lucky one.

The field around us was alive, so as Mum continued to fill up her saucepans, I explored its distractions. There were grasshoppers hopping, flowers to smell and pick, colors to identify. Colors were vivid that day and I knew colors! Sky was blue. Strawberries were red; their flowers white; their leaves green. Pale yellow sprigs of grass, already hay, stood up straight and tall. Bright yellow buttercups grew among the grasses. Yellow and white daisies grew near the ditch beside the road. Yellow butterflies flitted among the daisies as the yellow sun shone down on us, making the field golden in its warm rays as I twirled around and around in my favorite pale yellow dress, its hem dancing in the breeze.

What a perfect day!

These were my thoughts while pulling into the parking lot of the hotel as the golden yellow sun, high in the bright blue sky, again warmed the earth.

A field lay beyond this hotel where I was to stay during the fading days of my mother's life. In that field, I could see an expanse where light yellow grasses grew not very high, standing sparsely. It called out to me—called me to come discover its secrets, the insects, butterflies and buttercups, and, close to the ground, little white flowers and strawberries. It made me smile, deeply. Hidden in that field was all the wonder contained in those little wild berries. It was waiting.

And so it was that my mother, Priscilla, and I shared that day at sunset, the reddening of the sky glowing brilliantly through the window behind us, a magical bowl of those earthly wonders. She, like me, had spent hours with her mother in fields of wild strawberries. Each of us knew that strawberries, with their tiny seeds, were a forbidden fruit of her diet, but we also both knew that the remaining hours of her sensory enjoyment were becoming few.

When our two spoons scooped the last of those precious strawberries from the deepness of the bowl, our eyes met, smiles spread, faces softened. As we tasted the last of the berry burst of flavor lingering on our lips we both understood that we had simultaneously drifted to the memories of our beginnings.

What a perfect day!

A Dog's Life

Brianna Bleiwas

The house was empty. A strange vehicle pulled into our driveway, and my owner's daughter hopped out of the seat that I ride in when I go to the vet. She gave a strange man a hug. I wanted to run outside and jump on him, then walk away. Instead, he walked back to his vehicle and drove off, and my owner's daughter sped towards the door.

I approached her like I always do when she comes home, but for some reason, she was frightened. She's never afraid. Uh oh...did she smell the blood on my coat? She must have. She slowly walked to get me a treat- yay, treat! I led her to the box and waited not-so-patiently for the treat to be thrown to me. *Where's the treat? Where's the treat?* The box made a loud crumbling noise as she took out half a biscuit from the box. Yay, treat!

Suddenly, tears began to stream down her face as I went to lick her hand. Why was she sad? Did I do something wrong? I was just trying to defend my-self- the little girl poked me in the eye! I got closer and leaned against her, hoping to comfort her. Why shouldn't I? She just gave me a treat!

A couple of hours later, the little girl came home. Her face was stitched up, making her look like an old doll I chewed up that got repaired. I approached her, and she began to cry- but I licked her hand and she calmed down. They talked about how I was going to get to stay at home; they weren't going to give me away. It wasn't my fault, they said. The little girl provoked me. Yay, more treats! I grabbed my tug-of-war rope and handed it to the other girl. She gently played with me. At least I wasn't the only loyal member of that family.

Cousin James

Edward Ford

It was about one or two in the morning, on a hot summer night in Philly. There was this hard loud knock at the front door. Big Mom, my grandmother, raised the second floor front window and shouted,

"WHO IS IT?"

"It is me, Cousin James."

"I don't know-- a Cousin James."

"I'm James Osborne, Sue Osborne's third born son."

"My cousin Sue Osborne who lives in Neil's Cross Road, South Carolina?"

"Yes, Ma'am."

Big Mom then called to me, "Wake-up, Henry, your cousin James is downstairs. Go open the door."

Now, it is important to point out. This was Philadelphia, PA, having a population of over 2 million then in the mid-1950s or so. For a big city Philly wasn't too bad (just my opinion), but still it would be wise not to let anyone in your home at one or two a.m.

I went downstairs and opened the door. There stood an imposing man in his mid-20s who immediately gave me an overwhelming loving bear hug.

"How doing, Cousin? I'm James. What's your name?"

"I'm Henry."

Big Mom came downstairs. Cousin James and Big Mom began talking about James's trip, various relatives and South Carolina.

"How is your mother?"

"She is doing fine. Thank the Lord. Everybody is okay."

"The last time I saw you, you were a little boy. Now look at you. You are a big man now."

"THANKS!"

"Can I get you something?"

"No, Ma'am, I just need some rest."

There was a little more small talk. Then Big Mom said, "Henry, let Cousin James sleep in your room."

"Yes, Ma'am."

"You can sleep on the folding cot in the back room."

"Yes, Ma'am."

We woke up around 8:00 a.m. Big Mom fixed a nice breakfast (grits, eggs, bacon, scrapple, coffee, juice and biscuits). After eating, Cousin James went out to his station wagon, which looked like it was about to fall apart. He brought in several items which he gave to Big Mom. The items were gifts (clothes, a handmade quilt and food) from various relatives.

We talked until it was noon. I remember Cousin James saying to me:

"You have a nice a room; you have a lot of comic and regular books."

"Thanks. I like reading."

"That's very good. You keep that up. You will be very smart. I wish I had read more."

"I will."

"Well, I got to go now."

Big Mom and I walked Cousin James out to his station wagon. He had a road map showing that his final destination was New York City. He explained that he had a job that his brother there got for him. He started up the station wagon, resulting in a huge puff of smoke coming from the exhaust. The car's tires looked quite worn and about to go flat. Feelings of great concern rose for Cousin James because that station wagon didn't look like it would make it to the next block, let alone to the Big Apple, another 100 miles away.

Nevertheless, Cousin James was off, continuing his journey and what looked like to me a great adventure (I wanted to go with him). That was the first and last time I saw him; but, for me, Cousin James has an everlasting spot in my memory and heart, for such a brief encounter.

Her Cherished Place

Barbara Quint

She stood at the edge of the water in quiet contempla-
tion just as she had so many times before. The late
afternoon sun cast a brilliant yellow path across the
calm water. It seemed so far to the other side. Nearby, the brown ducks glided and dunked, tails straight
up. Their protector, with his gleaming teal head, kept
watch while his harem ate their fill.

Shirley had taken her here so long ago to feed the
hungry brood, gleeful as they bustled at her tiny feet.
How many generations of ducks ago was that?

She came as a school girl to this pond house with
its rough timbered floor and the wooden benches that
appeared every winter. She went there every weekday,
stayed all day weekends, pulling tight the laces of her
hockey skates. Oh, the disdain she had for those sissy
girls who wore figure skates! *You can't skate fast in those!*
All they did was make circles on the ice.

She loved the wintry afternoons she skated all
alone on the frozen pond, glimpses of pale sunlight
peeking through the trees at the far end, and the seren-
ity as she skated the hidden coves between the small
treed islands. What had seemed so far to go when water was just moments over ice.

She welcomed the older boy who appeared one

day, an unexpected mentor. What pleasure to skate with him in tandem! How she embarrassed herself by bragging how fast she could skate, clearly knowing he was better skilled.

Early spring, benches gone, the vast empty pond house became host for her and her neighborhood friends. They ran in circles and every which way, laughing and shouting. The crash! The pain! A head colliding at full speed with hers, crushing her nose.

She came to the pond with her pre-teen girlfriends just to be somewhere together. She came with Shirley and her family when they visited. She gathered with her friends in the large grassy area on the other side of the trees to flirt with boys from the prestigious junior high.

She rode her bike for hours on miles and miles of red clay roads that wound through magnificent woods. She remembered her fascination with hordes of azaleas growing wild alongside.

This is her beloved place, this pond, this bench, the pond house, the woods. It will always be her special place. She knows she will never travel back, but she can close her eyes and go there any time she wants.

Memories from Water

Sarah Gamarra

When people think about water, they may think about the beach. When I think about water, I think about rivers and lakes.

I'm the youngest of my family, so while everyone was at school, my mom and I would go on different adventures. The one that stuck with me the most after all these years is when my mother would take me to the river off of the Pedestrian Bridge in Albany. On our way to the river, I would try to find my family name on the bridge. I knew the general location of our name stone, but could never find it. Eventually, my mother would point out the stone's specific area and I would find it within ten seconds. After looking at the name stone and taking a mental image of the location and the picture that it's next to, my mother and I would continue walking down.

We'd get to the end of the bridge and walk next to the stairs that lead to the dock. I remember the first time I went with her, she acted like it was our secret spot. We walked down the stairs and I held her hand tight – as tightly as a five-year-old could do – in fear of falling into the river. After every time we went, I got more and more comfortable to the point where I would run the whole dock length. My mother and I would sit at the edge of the dock and look out at the Hudson. The best part of the river would be when a boat would come and the waves would vibrate off the boat and linger all the way to the dock, rocking the dock back and forth. It was like our own little rollercoaster.

Now when I go back I think of the times that my mother would take me there. Even though she can't be with me now, I cherish the memories that I do have and I love the river for it.

I went to school at SUNY Oswego and if you know anything about Oswego, it's that it has beautiful sunsets and it's on the shore of Lake Ontario. I was one of the lucky people that had the lake in my back yard. But I didn't think much about it my first few weeks there, until I met Jeremy. We lived a few doors down from each other and quickly became friends. I would usually get out of class before everyone else, and noticed that Jeremy would be in his room. Of course, we would hang out and wait till everyone got there to go to lunch. Eventually, this turned into Jeremy and me getting lunch together. We would sit at the high table and get a view of the lake.

On the days when we didn't have work to do and in desperate need of fresh air, Jeremy and I would go to the lake and sit down on the rocks. During the warmer months, the wind that came off the lake was welcomed. The water was a beautiful green-blue color and the sun beaming down on it caused a glare in some areas. The waves would crash against the rocks and recede back into the water to come back crashing into the rocks. While watching the waves, Jeremy and I would talk about easier conversations like our classes, which led to our high schools, which led to our hometowns and ultimately to more open and vulnerable conversations. But it was so easy to talk to each other. The words from our mouths flowed like the lake on calmer days. The conversations that we had were hard and impactful like the waves on the rocks, but at the same time, it was like we had known each other our whole lives.

Lake Ontario was where we went to talk about anything. The lake was where our friendship grew into a relationship, which grew into love. We would express our concerns about life at the lake and talk about our ambitions and dreams.

One time I woke up strangely early in the morning and texted him if he wanted to go to the lake and watch the sunrise. To my surprise, he texted back. We went out to the lake that morning and watched the sunrise and had our first kiss there.

I met my best friend at the lake. Now that we have both graduated, we still make a trip every year on our anniversary to visit the lake. It's funny to think that back then, we talked about our past at the lake; now we talk about our future and how we can't wait to bring our children to the lake to see where their parents met and fell in love.

Novel Excerpt

Harvey Havel

Along the border of Albany and Latham, the entrance to a large shopping mall stood beside a crowded route that unfurled into the country. The bar rested on a knoll that had its borders for nightlife clearly demarcated. The patios on each side of the bar let in the cool air. Younger, beautiful women crowded the place as though they had been waiting for a good suitor for the longest of times. Soon, they would get tired and wander away, thinking bars shitty places to meet men. For me? I just liked to look at these women.

I had very little courage to walk up to these women and talk to them back then. They had always arrived with company, and it became difficult to maneuver around their friends and barge into conversations, until, finally, the women wanted me gone. And then I wouldn't stop bothering these starlets and beauty queens, and the final step always involved a couple of bouncers who threw me out.

Luckily this all didn't happen yet, but I made sure not to bother anyone or make fools of them. It became priority number one to behave myself as I sat at the bar and ordered drinks. I must have drunk beer for a couple of hours straight, just one after the other. I loosened up and started to approach women. One of them must have complained, because what were once party havens now proved to be tricky waters to find someone to take home for the night. Bars, apparently, no longer catered to the much desired one-night stands. I had to sit alone and drink until I blacked out. The next thing I knew I was alone in my apartment unsure of how the night ended or how I got home. I just didn't remember. I couldn't remember anything.

I stayed in bed terribly hung over. I was sick and not thinking straight. I regretted even going to the Latham bar, but as the day stretched out, I did get a phone call. It was Gypsy. Her voice and her commitment to coming over that evening made me feel better. I had a little cash left for her. I had to spend it on her. I thought she'd cure my sickness from the night before. All I yearned for was my body, my sick, sweating body, melting into her soft skin and her willingness to do whatever I wanted. She treated me much better than any other time before after she undressed, as though I were a frequent flyer or had coupons and frequent flyer miles for the time spent with her, or a VIP pass of some sort. She must have missed me.

"Do you still want to marry me?" she asked as she got up to have a cigarette after making love to me.

"I'm all out of money, Gypsy. I have nothing left."

"Are you getting a job?"

"It doesn't look good from that angle either."

"I can't come back, Charlie. You would still have to pay for my services, whether you could afford it or not."

"If we got married? What then?"

"Do you really want to marry me? It doesn't seem like you're very serious about it."

"I just don't know anymore. Things have gotten so confusing for me. I don't know anything - what to do, what to wear, who to call. I just feel like sleeping a lot."

"Sounds like you're pretty damned depressed," she said.

"Yeah."

"Well, you have a lot to be depressed about. You just lost your job, your family said goodbye to you. Albany is a new place for you, and you want to have a family. I don't know either, Charlie. You've taken a dive. I don't know how to help you."

"You mean you actually want to help me? That's something new."

"Are you still going to work minimum wage?"

"I don't have anything else."

"What if I said that I can show you how to be rich?"

"I'd say, fill me in."

"I have friends who may be in need of some help."

"Doing what?"

"Selling drugs."

I chuckled here, because I had to. This is what my life had boiled down to.

"I'll wind up in jail."

"Maybe, but I think you're missing the point."

"Me? That I'll wind up in jail?"

"Charlie, don't insult my intelligence."

"For the last time, I am not trying to insult your intelligence."

"People are making thousands. If you sell crack or H, you at least have a chance. Tomorrow, I'll take you to some people around here that I know."

"It's already tomorrow. It's three in the morning."

"Sleep then. We'll have the afternoon and evening of tomorrow to get you hooked up, okay? Don't worry so much. Let's see what they say."

"Who's they?"

On Not Doing It:
An Emersonian Homily on Restraint

Edward Fagen

> *The manifestation of power which*
> *impresses men most is restraint*
> —Thucydides

Earl Scruggs, of the bluegrass team of Flatt and Scruggs, is undoubtedly the world's most famous banjo picker. His high-velocity pickin' style has never been equalled and is the envy of would-be imitators. One of these imitators was once heard to say, "I'd like to be able to do it - and then not do it." This man understands restraint, the touchstone of power, competence, and authority.

I first learned about restraint from fishing tackle. When I was about eight years old, my father bought my brother and me our very own rods and reels. At the time the undisputed king of the fishing reel business was the Pflueger Co. of Ohio. Pflueger made three freshwater casting reels, the 'Akron' at $5, the 'Summit' at $15, and the 'Supreme' at a breathtaking $25 (This was 1939.). My brother and I received Akrons. The shiny endpieces of the Akron reels were adorned with a few tasteful curlicues and organic spirals, almost certainly stamped rather than engraved at that price. The endpieces of the Summit were considerably more elaborate, engraved all over with a dense mass of herbal forms that looked like a bug's-eye view of an arboretum. Parts that hadn't been engraved were damascened, in the manner of a dashboard of a runabout. I wondered how ornamentation could be carried any further in the top-of-the-line Supreme. Father showed me his new Supreme. I was astonished to see that it had no engraving whatsoever. In fact it wasn't even shiny; it was a uniform gunmetal grey with softly rounded corners. And this was the Cadillac of casting reels! Pflueger understood not doing it, and after that, I did, too.

Years later, while rooting through my wife's pantry one day, I came across a canister I had never seen before, labeled 'Socialist Realist Bread Crumbs.' I opened it up out of curiosity and found it full of stale bread slices.

"These are not bread crumbs!" I complained.

"Of course they are," she replied. "I can see you have never read any socialist literature. They are already bread crumbs in my mind, because I am perfectly confident that I can make them into bread crumbs if I need to."

There is no better place to observe restraint than in the concert hall. The Chopin G minor Ballade Opus 23, concludes with a powerful coda of 54 measures. The coda is carefully prepared with a long interrogatory passage, pregnant with anticipation and mounting excitement. At the last possible moment the tempo is doubled and the coda itself bursts forth in a mighty downward gallop, marked *presto con fuoco*, "quickly, with passion." The dynamic marking is *ff*, "double fortissimo." With one exception, every pianist I have ever heard, including the great Rubenstein, plays this passage *presto che possible*, "as fast as possible," at triple fortissimo. What a splendid display of power and virtuosity! The exception is the now forgotten Robert Casadesus. When the dam breaks in the Casadesus recording, it does so in slow motion, first a hesitant trickle, then a gathering flood, then at last an irresistible torrent, still gathering momentum as it engulfs the listener. As small matter of artistic judgement, perhaps, but a little *rubato*, a little holding back, has transformed a breakneck chase into an elemental force of nature.

To know how to do it and then not do it; to be aware that one has the power and the competence and the authority, and then to choose not to exercise them; to prefer restraint to mastery and self-control to domination—this is a gift. How one wishes that the wisdom to hold back, of not doing all that one is capable of doing, had been given to the political leaders and technological masters of our age. What might we have been spared? Auschwitz? Dresden? Hiroshima? Chernobyl?

On-the-Job Training

Mary Kate Owens

As a student, I took the jobs I could get, as I found them, and did not consider them important. I don't know that if someone had told me to learn from these itinerant occupations— to work hard, be careful, fulfill my commitments, do well — would I have listened?

Forty-seven years ago I was a deputy housekeeping manager at a motel in Ithaca - I worked from 6 - 11 A.M., which fit with my schedule. The highfalutin title and the 25 cents more than minimum was because they figured a 'college girl' could "fill in"; if one of the housekeeping staff called in, I was deputized to clean their roster of rooms or do the cleaning audit. Most of the maids were developmentally delayed, and were very jealous of their responsibilities and did not like me nosing in. I mostly ran the laundry mangle with an older woman and we did a complicated dance, which ended with towels and sheets, tablecloths and napkins folded in neat packages. The room we worked in was hot and steamy, from pulling heavy loads out of the washing machine and putting them in the dryers; pulling them out still damp and running them through the mangle press; dancing and folding as a pair and putting them still steaming on the housekeeping carts or in the cloth storage bins. The job ended when my co-worker left and was replaced by a farm girl who was a born-again survivalist. She spoke openly of the time when a plague would come on city-dwellers and she and her family would arm themselves and survive on home-canned goods and poultry. I found her dystopic views upsetting and I missed my old friend who had danced more gently and freely with me when folding, so I quit. The manager asked me to stay, and told me he would fire the new girl, but I demurred. I fold sheets and towels and tablecloths now - a different dance than the one I knew - but the neat packages, folded in thirds, stay with me.

At about the same time, I worked as a dinner waitress for an executive group which was at the university for a seminar. One of the men - they were all men - was my brother's prospective father-in-law. He had met me earlier in the spring; now when he saw me and recognized me, he stood up and introduced me to the others at his table. I was terribly uncomfortable when he stood up - it was a courtesy gesture - and there I was in a shabby waitress uniform serving them. At another table, a man would stroke my backside each time I came near him to pour coffee or tea. One of the other girls told me to 'spill' the coffee in his crotch the next time he touched me, but I just avoided him. I was not brave or bold. Mary's father - my brother's fiancée's name was Mary - standing up for me gave me a feeling of self-importance that persisted beyond that summer job.

I was not a great waitress; I was willing but not skilled enough to anticipate my guests' needs. One summer at a resort in the Thousand Islands, I worked breakfast and lunch, which was the low-earning, low-prestige end of the schedule. On Sunday mornings, the reservists from Fort Drum would come in en masse for brunch and we would rush to serve them. I remember charging a soldier $8 for the individual components that he ate, rather than the special $6 rate for the combined elements. He asked me to correct it. Feeling overwhelmed by all the tables yet to be served, I said to him, "Were you going to tip me?" "Yes," he said. "Well, just forget the tip," I said. He tipped me anyway and I carry the shame of that moment.

Two well-to-do ladies came to lunch on Wednesdays and each ordered the same thing: a diet plate special - cottage cheese, fruit, a hard boiled egg - and a double old-fashioned, hold the fruit and bitters. I would order the old-fashioned from the bartender, who one week laughed and said, "Do you know what they're ordering? Hold the fruit and the bitters - that's straight whiskey!" I wasn't shocked; I was surprised that they were unwilling to order the whiskey straight; they seemed authoritative and assertive to me. I did not think then "Will I be like that when I'm their age?" I had no vision of myself as a grown up, much less an old woman. Today, I would order the whiskey. And I'd take the time to correct the tab. It did not occur to me then that these jobs would make me who I am today.

Other People's Windows

Sandi Dollinger

I come from women staring out of windows. My father's mother, my *Babcia*, would give a hundred strokes to her dough as she looked out our upstairs kitchen window onto the gray siding of Fran Weslow's house next door. Did *Babcia* see the Warsaw of her childhood, where her first love sent her handwritten poems on silky pages before she came to America? Or did she see a Warsaw on its knees, reduced to cinder and ash during the 'Rising of 1942'? One day in May of 1950, I brought her a Polish book from the Genesee Library. Little did I know that the book described the annihilation of her birth city, a city once described as *The Paris of the East*. *Babcia* began screaming: *"Warsawa is no more!"* I hurried the book back and never brought another.

And I remember Mama, sitting at her kitchen window downstairs, while she mended shirts and darned socks. Was it her own beloved father in his bakery that she was seeing? Or was it Tommy, her stepfather, as he yanked her from my father's car, dragging her back to his own bedroom inside their Walden Avenue home? The last time I saw her, Mama told me this story for the first time. She said the day after it happened, she took a bus to the Buffalo City Hall to report him, but when she got there, she turned around and came back.

Now I, too, stare out of windows. Not my own, a window in downtown Albany looking out onto the dark, dank wall of next door's brownstone. I look out other people's windows, where some feline charge and I enjoy watching finches, sparrows and cardinals succumb to the delights of bird feeders, while squirrels scramble beneath for leftovers. Perhaps, Dear One, you think me entitled, but I am merely grateful for a piece of graphite to remember it by.

Stars Behind Bars

Liz Lynch

Max plopped his notebook on the conference room table and sighed.

"I'm not expecting much from anyone," he said. "The other two auditions were just dreadful."

I tried to think of something encouraging. I couldn't.

Max wrung his hands. "I wonder if anyone will even show up. I emailed appointment times to them, but not a single person confirmed. Why are people so rude?"

I quietly said, "I think the kids text now…"

"Well, I don't do that," he said haughtily.

It was true. Max didn't text or tweet or take part in techie trends. Mastering email was his compromise and he'd be first to admit that he was out-of-step with most people. Max is akin to a 1920s man-about-town: charming, elegant, and very mannered. It mattered not that he was actually born decades after the '20s— something about that era grabbed his heart and his soul and never let go. Why else would he be casting for a silent film production?

Max straightened his bowtie and checked his reflection in the glass door. "I hope I don't get method actors," he groused. "That's simply not going to work here."

Moments later, a man poked his head in through the doorway. "Is this the audition?" he quietly asked.

"Come in, come in," Max welcomed him. The reticent actor was tall and slender, dressed more for barn work than for a leading man role. Max put him through the paces and then a succession of hopefuls appeared. Things seemed to be moving along nicely — so well, in fact that I considered cutting out for a smoke break. Just as that thought entered my mind, Max rushed over to me.

"I need you to audition," he said.

"What? I'm no actor."

"You're better than they are," he insisted. "At least you get it. They don't."

Max is my friend and I'd do almost anything for him. So I "auditioned." He directed me to contort my face, my gestures and my body. It wasn't too bad, but when he finished, I definitely wanted that smoke. So I went outdoors.

The room had a whole new set of actors when I returned. A diminutive woman stood out from the rest. She had a sparkle in her eyes and boundless energy. She could laugh, she could cry, she could instantly convey anything Max requested. She was a miracle.

Max immediately cast her for the female lead. In addition to her obvious talent and experience, she told Max that she could secure funding for him. Her film and television credits would also be good for publicity. Was this too good to be true?

I had to ask Max, "Why is she in Albany?"

"She's taking a break for the summer, but she wants to keep her acting skills sharp," he explained. "And she's taking some kind of workshops, too."

"What kind of workshops?" I asked.

"I don't know; it sounds like some new-age thing, I guess," he laughed. "She wanted me to check out one of their seminars — up in the suburbs somewhere."

Something seemed peculiar about this, but Max has a way of creating magnificence in the most unlikely ways from the most unlikely circumstances. The money he had secured for the initial shoot was quickly drying up. This gal assured him that she knew big rollers who would finance the film's completion. The gamble seemed worth it.

Still, I researched the organization. Local news accounts insisted her group was a cult, a cult that starved and branded women and did other dark acts. I mentioned this to Max and he laughed. "Don't worry. I'm not going to join up!"

Max started production. But when the leading lady was scheduled to work, her reasons for "no shows" were as extensive as her resume. Max shot around her as much as possible. But the summer season was closing in fast, making it impossible to match up the outdoor shots. Finally, she stopped answering phone calls or returning emails. Max had no choice but to re-cast her part and attempt to complete the film.

Soon we heard from other indie filmmakers in the area. Turns out our gal had auditioned, and secured, the leads in all of their films, too. She gave them the same promises. And she pulled the same vanishing act that she pulled on Max.

Life is filled with auditions. Sometimes we're on stage; sometimes we stage others.

These days our young actress and her colleagues are up for the role of a lifetime, auditioning before a Federal Court in Brooklyn. Will they convince an audience of 12 they meant no harm? Will polished soliloquies tell of enlightenment or cruel, sadistic torture?

The actress was good, but I don't think anyone is that good.

Vale, Oregon

Rob Williams

This was a most eventful day. After my departure from Picabo Street's home town, I went on to Boise, Idaho, and reunited with my cousin Chris, whom I had not seen since his mother's (my aunt's) memorial service a few years before. (Unfortunately, his wife was away with a friend.) Despite not seeing him except for circumstances surrounding family deaths, the Boise area suits him: he is enthusiastic about fishing and hunting for large and small game, of which there is an abundance here.

One idea I gleaned from Chris was an activity in which he helps facilitate fishing expeditions for a support group in which he volunteers. While fishing trips in Upstate New York may not be practical and very time-limited, there are numerous other activities like trips to baseball games or educational trips of mutual interest. The point is that meetings with peers are not just about illness but more positive interests.

So Chris and I enjoyed lunch together looking at a rather large mural of the landscape in front of his house (aka picture window) and catching up on family news. Unfortunately, his cat had to be sequestered due to Skeeter's presence, but Skeeter enjoyed romping in a large fenced yard with Chris's other canines and masticating on the local dog chews. I was lucky enough to have Chris come to find me and help me to depart. By pure coincidence, Chris knew of my whereabouts in Picabo Street's home town as he had been on the Nature Conservancy board for the area and has hunted and fished there in the past.

I wondered why: 1) in this part of the country the roadside signage is so inadequate, and 2) why the most expensive campgrounds are the least attractive. These are not the kinds of questions that win friends and influence people. So I satisfied myself with my own answers. Road signs do not have a high priority where there are few attractions. If you know where everything is, you don't need help to get there, visitors be damned. And campgrounds borrow from their surroundings, so Picabo Street's area lends itself to a facility that is already attractive, being clean and well-kept by staff.

Thus, the trail here featured numerous false starts and ample back tracking, the ineptitude of this driver notwithstanding. Skeeter and I were so tired that we could easily have slept by the curb, taking no note of the surroundings. There are advantages to being here. We are in our destination state and can almost smell the salt water. The weather is so agreeable that we need no heat and limited outerwear.

The Four Elements

Betsey Kuzia

Fire: Radiation is closest to it. Tamed fire in a new form. Five weeks. I go to St. Peter's Hospital, strip, hop on a table in a lead-lined room. Carefully positioned, I hold my breath for 45 seconds times two. The red laser beam marks the spot where the energy will kill any remaining cancer cells. Not actually fire but so much like it. I look burned in just a square area where the beams cook my chest wall. Fire.

Water: At 5AM the alarm goes off, triggering WAMC and Morning Edition. What horrible thing will Donald Trump have tweeted today? After my first breakfast, the paper and cat feedings, I head to the Y to swim. Locker room greetings, book reviews and talk lead me to the water. Not my beloved ocean at the Cape but a chlorinated pool welcomes me. I adjust my goggles and submerge. Meditating as I notice how many laps swum (about 36 is a mile) I think—or not. The water stills, calms me. I stretch, move through fluid space. Free, noticing the tension in my hands as it slowly dissipates. I move through the water and pray in my own prayerful way.

Earth: I dig in the humble ground that is the land I own. A small plot of Albany that no one else wanted. I am grateful for this space. Working the soil brings me closer to some kind of God. Flowers affirm this, roses that return year after year, the fragrance of lily of the valley, lilacs in the spring. Knowing my ashes will someday return to the soil and the sea, I love and fondle the earth when I can. Walk on it, revere it. Offer thanks for its presence in my world.

Air: I adore being surrounded by it. In space when I was free-falling from an airplane. Moving through light and heavy air as I carve up curves on my tw-wheeled iron steed. Salt air, air fragranced by good and not-so-good smells. I have the capacity to still breathe. That may not have been but it is. Be grateful to exchange breaths on this day. Many whom you knew and loved no longer have that opportunity. Feel the wisps of late summer breezes as this pen floats through space. Stop and breathe it all in. You are meant to still be here right now.

The Secret

June Hannay Kosier

As many people know, I have great difficulty keeping secrets. The story that I am about to tell you is one I managed to keep for a long time.

Mr. Reggie Brown was one of the dialysis patients. He would come to his treatments with a can of Planter's peanuts. Dialysis patients are allowed only 2000 mg of sodium per day, so the staff would often tell him, "You shouldn't be eating those peanuts, Brown."

Reggie would tell us about how he had met Dr. Hines, the chief nephrologist and our boss, when he was a medical student at Albany Medical Center. Reggie was an orderly there and since they were both black, he would give Dr. Hines some fatherly advice about certain situations. Back in the early 60s there weren't many black medical students and Dr. Hines had to pioneer through school.

Mr. Brown suffered from narcolepsy. While holding his needle sites, he would begin to tell you a story about Dr. Hines as a medical student and fall into a deep sleep mid-sentence. Five or so minutes later, he would wake up and continue the story right where he had left off. It was difficult not to laugh and even harder not to just smile. He would get very mad at us for doing this. He knew from our reaction that he had had another narcoleptic event.

One Friday, Reggie's dialysis access graft was not functioning well. It was decided that he would go to the operating room after his treatment to have it cleaned out. He was the only patient, and I was the only nurse left in the unit. I was holding his arm to stop the bleeding after the dialysis needles had been removed from his access arm when he told me:

"You have to take my peanut can home with you."

"How about I take it downstairs on my way out of the building and leave it on your bedside stand?"

"No, that won't do. I don't want it stolen."

"Nobody is going to steal your peanuts, Reggie."

"You don't understand. Open it up."

I removed the plastic top from the tin and what to my surprise was in it but a whole lot of money.

"What are you doing with all this money? Someone might steal it."

"That's why I want you to take it home. I trust you."

"Why do you have it in the first place?" I was afraid he would fall asleep again before I got an explanation.

"I like to give my grandson money when he comes to visit, and I never know when he is coming. I am trying to help him get through college."

"Do you want me to get fired? If someone finds out I took your money home, I would be out of here faster than you could say 'Jack Rabbit'. I have a daughter in college, you know."

"I won't tell, and if you don't tell, nobody will find out. I can keep a secret."

"But I can't. Somehow, they always leak out."

"Well, what are we going to do then?"

"I will call the registrar and he will put it in the safe."

The registrar did come to the unit and the three of us counted the money. There was $2007.23 in the can. We all signed paperwork and the registrar took the money downstairs after giving Mr. Brown a receipt.

Reggie put the receipt in the can and asked, "Now will you take this can home?"

I still told him no but promised to put it on his bedside stand as previously discussed. He also had me promise not to tell anyone his secret about the money.

Mr. Brown lived a few more years and always brought his peanut can to dialysis. Nurses would continue to say things like "Peanuts are full of sodium, Reggie, and you know you aren't supposed to have a lot of sodium." Or "No wonder you're thirsty, eating salty peanuts all the time."

He would just look at me and smile. Nobody ever noticed that I never chided him about the peanut can. We had our little secret and one, I am proud to say, I managed to keep until today. I told you I am no good at keeping secrets.

The name of the patient in this story has been changed to maintain his privacy.

The Back Room

Ardelle Castellana Hirsch

I've arrived early for lunch, of course, but I'm glad to be in this space. It's beautiful; everything looks pretty and smells good. Candles on the tables, art on the walls, centerpieces creatively curated, gentle sounds, soft lights. Soon, someone beneath the calibrated "How're we all doin' today?" voice brings warm, grainy rolls and sweet tea. "Sparkling water or tap?" Then off to the back room, through the Employees Only door; it's different in there, in the Back Room.

A three-inch gap reveals a chaotic space: stainless steel, small and loud. It smells like burnt crème brûlée and looks like a ballet on steroids. Carrot skins stick to an oily rag on the floor and someone in a beet-stained apron is screaming about pesticides placed too close to cans of pearl onions. Out front, Spotify playlists and truffle oil-infused fries spill happiness to infinity and beyond.

At the table, wearing nice clothes, I spill happy stories and pleasantries with precisely picked words, but hit Control-Alt-Delete before getting to the rest. We eagerly share the sliced grainy rolls, but no gritty family secrets at this table, thank you very much. The unsaid things are over there, behind that door around the corner, one flight up. Decisions, decisions. My disembodied, internal voice asks, "Accuracy or Approximation today?" before disappearing through the cerebral swinging double doors: No One Permitted Beyond This Point. A devilish dichotomy.

Out front, it's all about the presentation, but there's always a Back Room. What we see, don't see; say, don't say; share, don't share; know, don't know: separate rooms for all.

After lunch, at the vet's office, the over-lit reception area is stuffed with outdated glossy magazines and fake flowers, just ten feet from those excrement encrusted cages and fear-filled whimpering things behind that door over there: Authorized Personnel Only. Closed off, clandestine, no windows in there - optimism floating on dirty sponges and sterile needles while sliding steel drawers carry Lysol-laced cold, heavy things: Keep Out.

And we do. We roll through red lights, pilfer pens, share Netflix passwords, but we don't ever go through those doors. Ever. We often send our representatives to check in, and then quietly check out, but we Do Not Enter that off-limits place where keys can't unlock open doors. Honestly, do you want to have a look or not?

The best stories are housed in the Back Room, fastidiously functional, and not so artfully displayed: The Real Deal. And not just in the external spaces but in the internal places, too. The inside outside upside downside places behind the I-Can't-Tell-You-That door. But I'd like to get to know you, not your representative. And I often struggle with what to share and with whom, how much, and how soon. I usually try to let it rise, like those yeast-filled soft rolls. But I'm awkward and impatient and eager to share. "How's your life?" I ask to avoid the automated, unrevealing, "Fine-thank-you-how-are-you?" exchange. "So what's your story?" I want to know. I'm glad to share my story as well; I've always preferred the authenticity and color found in the Back Room.

On the way home, a quick stop at the food store. Lackadaisical, aromatic Easter lilies show off and nod, lapping yellow yolky things unintentionally dribbled on tender, newborn basil leaves. The red and green peppers keep to themselves in their own bins out front, but on the other side of those swinging double doors, at the end of Aisle 3, box cutters tear into crushed cardboard boxes filled with rotting food; squishy red and green peppers with soft black spots collide. Fat, whiskered rodents lic in wait, folded dreams falling flat on the floor.

Just on the other side of the red velvet ropes, near the heavy windowless doors, privileged key-carrying, badge-wearing, apron-clad, sterile-gloved others push past the heavy doors. Richly scented spices are stored next to delectable dreams, valued heirlooms and slithering shame. Denial, visible and inaccessible, is hung on a rusty hook ten feet from the floor in the rooms without the candles: Authorized Personnel Only.

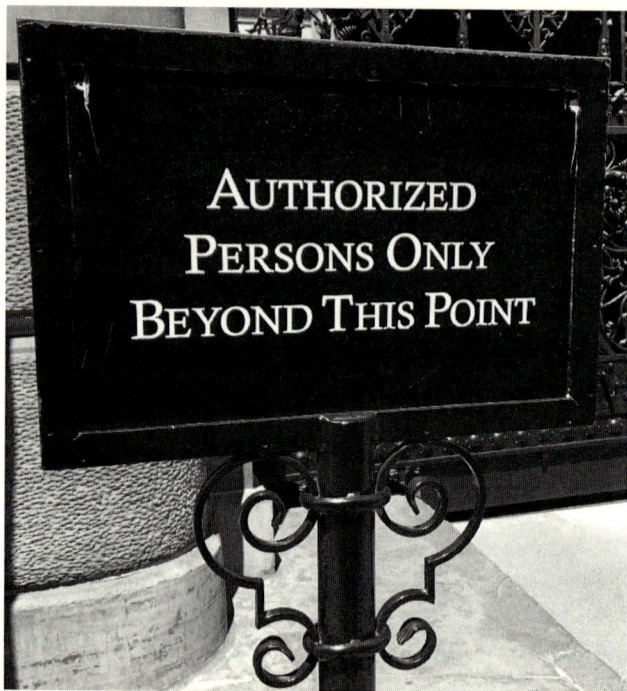

Letter from Albany, June 4, 2008

Barbara Kaiser

A quirk in the weather has affected the rhododendron
    bushes in an
alarming way. They are exploding all over town. Each
    bush is covered
with so many blossoms the leaves become invisible.
They look like clown bushes. They look surprised, happy and
embarrassed all at the same time.
I have never recalled in my entire life seeing anything like this.
I don't know what to make of it.
Meanwhile, earlier this spring, the rabbits ate the heads off
    most of the parrot tulips.
The season was mainly a disappointment with headless
    stalks abounding.
We killed two hydrangeas last summer.
The poppies are finally showing their orange heads after
    a long wait.
The white beach plums are blooming and we are expect-
    ing some very
hot weather in the 90s to scorch everything.
And what can we do about it? Nothing!
Oprah has Justin Timberlake on.
Just who I wanted to watch on this cloudy, rainy, humid day.

The Mad Tea Party

Barbara Kaiser

We were appalled, appalled
that you sat down.
All of us were appalled, appalled
that you sat down.
We told you to bring a chair,
We told you.
And you sat down.
You sat down.

You are uninvited
to our next repast.
Uninvited.

And you are no longer
our friend.
Because we were appalled
that you sat down.

(This poem is based on an actual
incident in which there were more
people than seats and I sat down.)

Grandma's Pie Shop

Barbara Kaiser

Instead of
"Today, Cinnamon Apple"
the sign on Grandma's Pie Shop
right on Central Avenue
for everyone to see
read: "So long, Lenny.
Good luck."
Why is Lenny leaving?
Who will miss him?
It makes me feel sad.
Lenny, don't go!

Rearview Mirror

Pat Steadman

6/16/2019 (10/02/2017)

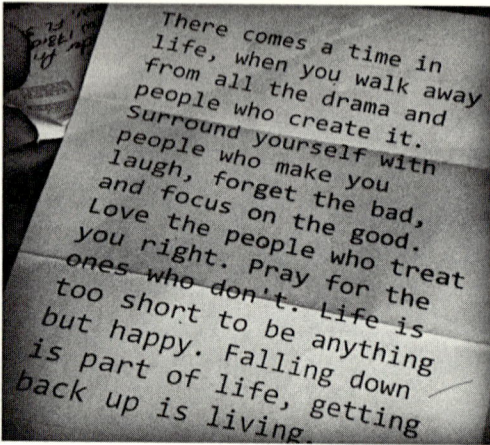

There comes a time in life, when you walk away from all the drama and people who create it. Surround yourself with people who make you laugh, forget the bad, and focus on the good. Love the people who treat you right. Pray for the ones who don't. Life is too short to be anything but happy. Falling down is part of life, getting back up is living.

I received this posting on my Facebook page a year ago. Like so many of these anonymous postings of "spiritual awakening," I ignore them but this one had a tiny hammer attached to it and a small chip in my armor was chinked. Little did I know how the past nine months would play out, but I kept going back to this writing I saved to my flash drive.

Three years ago I desperately wanted to get out of the apartment building and city I had lived in for the past fourteen years. I felt like a prisoner in my "home," leaving almost on a daily basis for six or more hours to escape to any library where I could do genealogy research on my family or just get lost in the inner sanctum of the internet.

I started going to "open houses" of newly-built 55-and-older retirement communities, and found myself going faster and faster down the rabbit hole of desperation and depression. I could never afford these realtor fantasies of retirement life, and even if I could afford them, I wasn't going to substitute one controlled environment with another. I was brought up in houses, two to be exact, where I wasn't told how to live, what and when to eat, how to fill my days up with annoying strangers participating in daily activities I had no desire to be involved in. I knew I would never be able to purchase a house, to have a small piece of property for a garden and an old dog to live with, four-legged, not two-legged: that was all I wanted. I needed out of the city and its problems. I started filling out applications to various apartment buildings that were smaller, accepted subsidies, and were out of the city—and I heard nothing.

During those past three years I would drive a distance in every direction away from Albany constantly praying to God for what I thought I wanted: peace, quiet, country, no major highways. I wanted mountains, to watch a sunrise or sunset and the colors of the skies over the mountains. I wanted water—my astrological sign after all is Cancer, a water sign; when I lived in San Jose, California, I lived between the San Francisco Bay and the ocean and was never happier.

An ocean was out of the realm of possibilities but I wasn't looking to live in a flood zone either. I also got introduced by a librarian to author Louise Penny and her mystery writings about a fictional small village south of Montreal near the Vermont border, that no one ever heard of and wasn't located on any map or GPS system, called "Three Pines." So, in my ritual driving and prayers I wanted to find Three Pines to live in.

Back at the beginning of the year I was diagnosed with cancer and treated with surgery. I never felt physically ill but the mind and emotions turned many a sunny day into darkness. I had never before experienced the positive energy I needed from the support and prayers of this wonderful writing group that I clung to in my darkest hours. Another milestone: I turned seventy. Then, in July, I was contacted by two apartments out of several I had applied to three years ago. One told me I was eleven on their list and it could be another year or two before a vacancy would be available; the second one told me a vacancy was available in September. I asked what would happen if I chose not to take the vacancy now and was told I would be put on the bottom of the list and the wait would now be five years. Sight unseen, with no knowledge of the area or the building, on blind faith, I said yes.

After a month of moving in, tired, sore, I never felt so at peace and at home. Looking out the window one evening I realized I got everything I prayed for. While I didn't find Three Pines, Three Pines found me. A fresh start.

An M & M Christmas: 1954

Kathleen McCabe

By no means were we a well-to-do family. Our home was humble and we were on the lower end of middle class. Some may have judged us as poor. But, to the credit of my mother and father, we children never felt that we lacked anything, or that our needs were not met.

Activities that gave us great pleasure, such as tobogganing on the slopes of the snow-covered golf course at Frear Park, skating on Cooper's pond, and taking rides through the fancy sections of the city to look at Christmas decorations were some of the adventures that Dad would organize. These activities were great fun and cost nothing, and left us with the indelible gift of time spent with our dad.

Our home consisted of several small rooms and it was occupied by Mom, Dad, seven children and my father's brother, Uncle John. The house had been a two-family, but when the upstairs neighbor passed away, Dad converted most of those rooms to sleeping quarters.

Mom was expecting again, with her due date in mid-January. She was pregnant with twins. One may think this a shock to parents who already had seven, but early in the pregnancy Mom's doctor thought he heard three separate heart beats. So the news of twins actually came with a bit of relief to my parents.

As Christmas approached each year, it was a ritual for us siblings to browse the Montgomery Ward catalogue and choose most of our gifts, particularly the toys. I do not recall the details, but I know that Mom and Dad had some convoluted explanation as to how Santa could make our gifts, but they also could be listed in the store's catalogue.

We always had a real tree, purchased from a local merchant, and we would decorate it with large colored lights, glass ornaments and tinsel. On Christmas Eve we would excitedly hang our stockings on the mantel. They varied in color, length and size, many coming from my sister Pat's collection of argyle knee socks. We looked forward to the contents we would find there in the morning, usually an orange, an apple, some nuts and a candy cane. Such was our holiday preparation, and there was always great anticipation of what the big day would bring.

As wonderful as previous ones had been, it was this particular Christmas in 1954 that stands out as my most memorable. Early that morning, Dad came to each of our bedsides, gently waking us and giving us the news that we had two new baby sisters, one born at 2AM, the second one at 2:06. We asked how this could be, since Mom was not due for a few weeks. Dad explained that sometimes twins come early. My joy was such that I felt like I could not contain it. I hopped out of bed, blurting, "I have to tell Dee and her mom and the Fitzpatricks and Maureen Murphy."

Our household was aglow that morning, with much chatter about such things as what will their names be, what do they look like, how much do they weigh? In those days there were no ultrasounds, so women did not know a baby's sex until the end of the pregnancy. Since Mom and Dad already had five daughters and two sons, they felt sure that these babies were going to be boys.

Later that morning, as I skipped happily around my block to announce the news, I remember getting some strange suggestions for names, since this was such a divine event, not only the birth of twins, but twins born on Christmas! *"How about Carol, you know, like the holiday songs?"* *"What about Noel or Star, in honor of the baby Jesus?"* Of course, that ultimate decision was not ours to make, and Mom and Dad settled on Mary Christine and Margaret Carol-nothing to do with holiday tunes, but simply two good Christian names.

In those subsequent days I learned that Mom had been sitting at her sewing machine that Christmas Eve. It was around 11PM. She was putting those last-minute touches-snaps, sashes, trim on the new doll clothes that she had made for me, when she had to abruptly stop and take that unexpected trip to the hospital.

As I sat beside our shimmering tree later Christmas Day, dressing my doll in a peach-colored frock with sash and puff sleeves, I barely noticed that there were button holes, but too few buttons on the back of the dress, or that some of the snaps were missing from dolly's blue velvet coat. I hummed a Christmas tune, and imagined Mom, sitting in her bed at the hospital, holding my tiny new sisters, smiling warmly as she looked from one to the other.

I Sat Instead of Walking

Huldah Thompson

I sat instead of walking because
I was tired of walking on the hard dirt street
I wanted to dip my feet in the cool trench water
I wanted to feel the cool shade of the trees
I wanted to swing on the swinger under the house
Because I wanted to close my eyes and just think

I sat instead of walking because
They, the old ones, were tired of walking
Because they can only sit and talk now
Because they have walked the walk
Because I needed instruction and guidance from them
Because I wanted to listen to the stories of their lives

I sat instead of walking because
I wanted to hear of their days in the rice fields under
the hot sun
I wanted to hear of the rainy season that threatened to
wash everything away
I wanted to hear about the many battle scars in the
Bauxite mines
I wanted to hear of their battles with alligators,
anacondas, and wild boars
I wanted to hear of their hopes and of their dreams

I sat instead of walking because

I wanted to see them laugh in their old age

I wanted to hear them reminisce over the trials of raising a family

I wanted to hear of the victories over typhoid, measles, mumps, and growing pains

I wanted to hear of their heart breaks, of mistrust and of trust assured

I wanted to hear their stories of God as their first and last hope for survival and answers

So I sat instead of walking because in doing so

I began to understand how precious my people are

I began to understand the rich heritage they have given me

I began to understand the joy, hope and pain of living

I began to understand that sweetness of life in spite of the struggle

I sat instead of walking because I now can see

How wonderful it is just to sit and have conversation with others who cannot walk

Training

Huldah Thompson

What kind of a housewife will you make!
With this kind of cleaning, this kind of cooking, and
that kind of washing?
No good man keeps a dirty wife or a woman for long.
You've got to know how to do these things properly.
If you don't learn now, you gonna pay for it later on.
Listen to me, I am doing my best to show you how to do
things the proper way.

I don't know where *yu* head is!
Remember to always strain the tea before serving it.
There is a right way to make fried bake, roti, and bread.
Rice is cooked loosely, not left in the water to soak and
end up lumpy.
Stew is never to be too hot with pepper or too salted.
Always wash your fish with lime or lime leaf before
adding the seasoning.
I don't know where you got that heavy hand with de salt!

When washing clothes, you must scrub them properly.
Iron you clothes before wearing them on the street;
It's improper to walk next to a good man with wrinkled
clothes.
And always put starch on the sheets, pants, and uni-
forms.

Scrub yourself properly with a piece of cloth or a piece of *nenwa*

Remember to put a cork full of Detal in the bathwater on Saturdays.

No man wants a wife who does not clean herself properly.

Oil your skin with fresh coconut oil so it remains soft and smooth

That way you will be more attractive to a husband

Comb that short hair, God knows it's not much but you can still try and keep it neat.

Stop that laughing, with all your teeth hanging out, only fools laugh like you do.

Pay attention to house work instead of staring into the sky like *yu na* get sense.

But Mummy!

"What if me na want a husband or decide to have more than one husband?"

"What if me want fo be like Miss Annie who owns her own place across the street?"

Miss Annie!

Miss Annie! *She na happy!*

She is a barren lonely woman who pretends to be happy!

Is that the kind of happiness *yu* want to have?

I see! This is the thanks I get for trying to train you to be a good wife.

The sky is falling pouring rain

Francine Berg

The sky is falling pouring rain
    sharply spiking small explosions
staccato on the large puddle
    side-saddling the wall of the warehouse.

Quiet after the trucks unloading their cargo inside
    having gone
and cutting skirts of water
    zig-zagging along canals across the black asphalt
washing the dust and oil floating tumbling
    the visual cacophony outside my window.

Kinetic energy where the rain streaks the ground
    pointillism bursts of gray rupturing the
puddles' calm
Liquid fireworks snap crackle pop
    If that way is up how come rain drips down?

The painted warehouse poles sparkle black and white
    stripes
standing guardian to the low-lying terrain
    softened by its own wet mirror surface
reflecting the thunder clouds white flying by

Lush summer green growth by my window
      enjoys the showering pour
Drips shine everywhere reflecting the twilight
      rivulets now still in the aftermath of the deluge
Wet is the word and it connects everything
      H2O gave us a show downpour and up-soak rain
Biosphere's ablution shalom amen

Spare Room

Francine Berg

I go outside to the clothesline.

I am all set to hang the clean, wet laundry.

I am in my spare room. It's the place I find twenty
minutes of cherished time to hang the clothes.

I find myself, with much laundry to do.

I lift the clothes, piece by piece. I open each
clothespin, place each strategically with my
hands and
fingers that open and close.

Music to me, the sound of the pins, the breezes,
the clean, aromatic laundry drying.

I am a lucky duck, in my spare room I am filled
with sun, breeze, the voices of children at play.

I am a child at play, filled on this sacred day,

Renewed in my spare room.

My Affair

Mary Clement

I am having an affair. And like any affair, I imagine, I am treading in dangerous and murky waters.

In denial at first, thinking I was just flirting around, I saw no harm in playing a bit, having a little fun. How could something so exhilarating be wrong? But now things have escalated. Quickly!

I had arrived at a spot of transition in my life, with new- found time in my days. I was beginning to think about me for a change. I was exploring new avenues.

But then somewhere along this road, I got lost.

Now, I'm forever scrambling to find time for much else in my life. I am distracted when forced to converse with my husband, and sweet children too. It doesn't occur to me to feed anyone until hours have passed by normal mealtimes and I've already ab- sently allowed them to fill up on whatever junk they could find for themselves. I've lost my pride, doing the very least I can to make it appear that I am keep- ing house; I spray the tubs and let the chemicals do the rest, give the toilet seats a quick pass with a Chlo- rox disinfecting wipe, briskly sweep crumbs and dust bunnies under nearby furnishings…now and then… if that. I order pizza repeatedly because the fridge is bare, pay bills after the due dates, let the machine answer all my calls, put the laundry in the washer, throw it in the dryer and then back into the basket, and I lie about where I've been and what I've been doing. It's disgusting, but I can't stop myself.

I never imagined I would have an affair. I am, by nature, pretty conservative, a bit of a prude really. I could never fathom being unfaithful, even if I tried. I thought loyalty was most important, devoted commitment, sacred. But now I'm having a full fledged, no holds-barred, all-out, wholly obsessive affair...... with writing!

I enrolled in a memoir class and now all I am moved to do is write. Even without pen in hand, even away from my computer, I'm writing in my head, nonstop composing of sentences, rearranging of words, and noting of new ideas. I snatch crayons to scribble across my children's artwork, on napkins, old envelopes, and dusty recipe cards; words come rushing in waves faster than I can record them.

I have become intimate with Webster. I take him to bed; I take him in the bathroom. I can't bear to be separated. His dictionary, his thesaurus, his grammar, usage, and punctuation guides are like nourishment. Drooling over his references, I devour the pages.

I steal time from errands to get lost in the book store. Then, drunk on the scent of freshly printed ink, minutes become hours and a teeny fib about tons of traffic becomes a big, fat, lie about a little old lady crossing the street who needed help, not only crossing, but getting home too, and then into her apartment, and feeding her cat, and making her dinner, and because she was so lonely, I just had to stay and eat with her.

And sleep? There's no sleeping! Three weeks in, I'm dreading the completion of this class. I want more. I want a "commitment" for more of the same, and a variety of others pertaining to any and all writing.

I am taxed with justifying paying for more courses while not getting paid for my efforts. I'm under the gun to learn how to change ramblings into comprehensive essays suitable for public radio, newspapers, or magazines, and story ideas into novels. Furthermore, I'm dismayed that there were no warnings listed in the course description.

Seasoned writers, where do you suggest I go from here? How long might this affair last? I think my children will get over my absenteeism, as long as I get myself back on track. I suspect I'll be able to charm my husband with a few well scripted notes, but frankly I'm scared. This new vice has quite a grip, wrenching me in ways unlike anything I've ever experienced before.

Someone suggested a therapist.

I'm going to give him a call just as soon as I finish this writing. Maybe he'll agree to meet with me, at my favorite corner table in the Starbuck's where I go to write.

Contributors

FRANCINE BERG always has a pencil. She is a writer. She has poems and stories to tell.

BRI BLEIWAS is a poet, blogger, and creative writer from Long Island, NY. In addition to running a mental health blog (briannafae.com), she is a ghostwriter for other bloggers. Bri is working on a poetry compilation that will be self-published by Amazon. She has also been published on The Mighty, a platform with perspectives on mental health and chronic health conditions.

MARY CLEMENT, a With Pen in Hand member since its inception, has been featured on WAMC Public Radio's Essay Spot, published in the Albany Times Union, and selected as a Top Ten Pick. She was an award winner for two essays appearing in the HVCC Literary Journal, and was selected to attend the NYS Writers Institute Community Writers Workshop. She earned a BFA with Honors in Creative Writing from SNHU. Mary lives in Albany with her husband, Jerome; she is the mother of eight children.

DIJONNAYE DANIELS is a disabled African American woman who, aside from writing poetry and plays, is a contributor to a local Albany newspaper called The New Scene.

PIERRE DESIR is a retired professor of cinematography and film production, who has traveled the world and loves meeting new people. He lives in Westerlo, NY, and spends his time writing, painting, sculpting, dreaming and cutting grass

SANDI DOLLINGER is a playwright and teacher/artist living in downtown Albany, NY. Last summer her play "Under the Aguacate Tree" was produced at Players' Ring in Portsmouth, NH. This past winter, her play "The Great Lithuanian Bake-Off" was staged as a dramatic reading at the Fenimore Art Museum in Cooperstown., NY. When not writing or teaching, Sandi enjoys traveling and the company of cats.

NANCY DUNLOP is a poet and essayist who resides in Upstate New York. She received her Ph.D. at UAlbany, SUNY and happily taught there for over 20 years. A finalist in the AWP Intro Journal Awards, she has been published in a number of print and digital journals. Her work has also been heard on NPR.

EDWARD FAGEN is a retired professor of physics and electrical engineering. He has enduring interests in classical music, sound reproduction, and steam engines.

EDWARD FORD WOW! Ed Ford is here to say he jumped in, is leaning forward, is moving and not looking back because he don't want to turn into a pillow of salt. Assuredly, a key to this is take one breath after another (Please! don't try to take two).

SARAH GAMARRA loves writing and reading books. Besides that she loves hanging out with friends and family.

KATE GLEASON, an inaugural member of With Pen in Hand, is a fiction writer and poet from New York City's West Village. Her writing has appeared in *Chrysalis, Iskra/Spark*, and other small press publications. She published the arts magazine *Lusty Mover: where art makes love* and curated the group shows *Beauty: Now You See It* and *Using My Religion*. She earned an MFA in Writing from Columbia University's School of the Arts. Her writer's haven is still the mobile home in Selkirk.

FAITH SWINGLE GREEN is a retired special education teacher who has been writing poetry for many years. She has recently branched out into memoir and flash fiction. She lives in the Capital Region with her cat, Belle.

HARVEY HAVEL lives in Albany, New York, with his pet cat, Marty. His is the author of seventeen books, including novels, a collection of short stories, and other writings on current affairs and political matters. All of his work may be found on *amazon.com* or *barnesandnoble.com*, or type in "Harvey Havel" into any search engine His books can also be purchased at your favorite local bookstore by special order.

ARDELLE CASTELLANA HIRSCH is a lifelong writer of memoir, poetry, essays, creative nonfiction, with very long "to do" lists. She is especially grateful to be actively involved in "With Pen in Hand." Prior to retiring, Ardelle worked in broadcasting, education and public affairs. Presently, Ardelle enjoys cooking too much food for her family and friends, dancing, photography, traveling - and crossing things off her very long "to do" lists.

REGINA "INDI" LACY (JONES) is a freelance writer/poet originally from Aberdeen Proving Grounds, Maryland; a single mother of 4 Sons: Rodriek, Garry, Elijah & Hezekiah. Regina began her writing at the early age of 7 when she penned her 1st piece on the palm of her hand. Regina is a great fan of Dr. Nikki Giovanni, who she has spoken with over the telephone. Regina has already done studio time where she wrote and produced her first Spoken Word CD "FrÊÊ NdÊÊd". - with many more under her belt. Regina has participated in the Capital District Artist Network, winning her first Award.

BARBARA KAISER is a poet, actress, writer whose work includes writing and producing the play "Locked in the Ladies' Room," which was performed off-Broadway at LaMaMa, etc., in New York City. Barbara recently performed in "The Vagina Monologues" in Albany. She has also been a long-time Jazz DJ at WRPI in Troy. Barbara is at work on a book of poetry and a new play.

ROBERT KNIGHTLY, a criminal defense lawyer Upstate, retired New York City policeman, and former NYC Legal Aid Society criminal trials lawyer, relocated to Albany 10 years ago from NYC, where he was born. Severn House (England) published his two crime novels; Akashic Books (Brooklyn) published "Queens Noir," a collection of original crime stories he edited; and six of his short stories have appeared in anthologies. In 2004, he sold a pilot script to Aaron-Spelling TV Productions and NBC (and got a free trip to Hollywood).

JUNE HANNAY KOSIER has been a nurse for over 50 years. She has never had a job that wasn't nursing or nursing related. She considers it a privilege to have cared for our nation's heroes for over 34 of those years at the Albany VA Medical Center.

BETSEY KUZIA is a Jack-of-all-trades (social worker, art therapist, motorcycle rider coach, and the TSA's favorite ukulele player). From clinical narratives to personal memoir and stories, writing is Betsey's way to reflect, slow down and leave a legacy.

PAUL LAMAR teaches writing and literature workshops in various libraries around the Capital Region, reviews theater for The Daily Gazette, and accompanies two choruses. He lives with his husband, Mark, in Albany, NY, not far from three grown children and two grandchildren.

JOE LEVY is a laid-back geek who is passionate about games, guitar, helping people, Jeet Kune Do, social justice, and his wife. He has interests in cooking, computer programming, hiking, rationality, recreational mathematics, and sci-fi/fantasy. He occasionally makes comedy music videos, and accepts payment in sushi.

LIZ LYNCH is a writer, artist, web designer, occasional radio guest, and most recently, a ukulele player. Her favorite passage in the Bible is "God hath chosen the foolish things of the world to confound the wise," which she feels describes her perfectly. Her contribution to this collection showcases just one of the many foolish things in which she has been involved.

KATHLEEN MCCABE is a retired Supervising Community Heath Nurse. She loves to read fiction, and to write memoir and humorous rhyme. Many of her pieces come from her experiences growing up in Troy, in a large Irish Catholic family.

SILVIA MIOC has always been an avid theater, music, dance and visual arts lover. Over the last couple of years she has focused on growing her creative and spiritual sides, re-inventing her life through yoga, meditation, writing, and painting. This has energized and awakened her to the true nature of peace and happiness.

JOSE MORALES was raised in New York City by working-class parents who were born in Puerto

Rico. He graduated from Iona College in 1969, where he majored in Spanish. After a long career in education, he retired in 2003. Since then, he has immersed himself in artistic endeavors: performing with local choruses; learning to oil paint, which culminated in a one-man exhibit in 2015; and writing, which he peppers with Latino inflection.

MICHAEL O'FARRELL is a graduate of The College of St. Rose and lives in Albany , NY. Retired, he worked for several years as a patient care technician. He is a confirmed movie buff and enjoys writing about films. Other interests have included acting, reading, listening to classical music and working on a memoir of his boyhood and adolescence.

JOAN OLIVER is a first-generation college graduate. Joan's blue collar ancestry provides the backdrop for a lifetime pursuit of literature, culture, art and philosophy. This juxtaposition creates a constant tension that informs her poetry and drawings. She maintains a studio in Glenmont, NY, with her Schnoodle, Scupper, where she draws, stitches, writes and teaches. Joan's poetry and abstract art portray her process to integrate and illustrate a lifetime of esoteric study against a lifetime of creative endeavors in multiple locations. "Energy of Place" - virtual and actual - informs an archive of poetry, drawings, prints, and textiles that are being readied for publication.

MARY KATE OWENS is retired from the NYS Unified Court System and has been a member of the Howe Memoir group for more than 3 years. Her primary writing interests are narrative non-fiction. She is also a gardener, a reader and a cook.

BARBARA QUINT is writing a memoir of her family starting several generations before she was born and continuing through her life. Her purpose in writing this family story is to let those who follow her learn of the personal lives and cultures that influenced those who went before.

EILEEN O'DEA ROACH—a devoted genealogist— recently finished her full-length memoir, <u>An Orchid for a Silver Lining: If the Kitchen Table Could Talk</u>. A retired labor union legislative assistant, she lives in Albany with her husband, Willis, and enjoys gardening. Her essay in this book is dedicated to her parents, Leo and Julia O'Dea, native Newfoundlanders, who taught her the value of family.

STEPHEN ROBERTS loves to write poetry along with books. Stephen is one half of the host team for the Troy Poetry Club and you can find the Troy Poetry Club on Facebook. Stephen has a poetry website: http//stephenspoetryworld.wordpress.com

ANNE ROKEACH is a resident of Colonie and a contented transplant from rural Maine. She brought her love of the outdoors to the Capital District, which has also offered her the arts and continued education. New to writing, the prose she shares is the beginning of her memoirs.

MARY PERRIN SCOTT, a writer of memoir, poetry and political commentary for The Albany Times Union, has published three books of poems and two books of memoir. An artist who works in watercolor and acrylics, she is currently illustrating the Psalms.

KEN SCREVEN is an award-winning television news journalist who retired in 2011 after 34 years at WRGB-TV. After several years doing radio news, in 1977 Ken became the first African-American man hired to do television news in the Capital Region. Ken was known for his 'personal' and 'humane' take on his news reports. He also wrote a popular blog on the Times Union website entitled "Off Camera Perspectives." Ken is contemplating writing a memoir. He resides in Albany's Center Square neighborhood.

JUDY SPEVACK found self-expression as a writer, artist, and actor. She sought out personal connections with her positive, optimistic and joyful expression of life. These qualities, which saw her through great loss during her early years, are what many people remember most about her.

PAT STEADMAN is enjoying retirement in a small, quiet village. She's involved in wood burning, painting, memoir writing and photography classes. She continues research in genealogy and plans a trip to Germany this year to meet with family for the first time.

SHARON STENSON has lived in upstate New York for much of her life. Sharon taught in the English Department of Schenectady County Community College. She is a widely published poet, a playwright, and a musician. Her play **Cantata for Two Voices and Horn** was presented as part of the Playwrights' Showcase at Albany Civic Theater and Conkling Hall in Rensselaerville. Sharon's book **Up On Mineral Springs Road** was published in 2018.

HULDAH THOMPSON is a producer, writer/storyteller who loves to write fiction, non-fiction, profile stories, along with essays and poetry. When given the opportunity to verbally tell a story, she is known to take a character from the Bible or from the pages of her real life and spin an alluring tale of intrigue and insight for her listeners.

JEAN VAN DYK writes memoir, short stories and poetry. She is a mother, a grandmother, an avid reader and occasional painter who lives in Slingerlands, NY, and Lake Worth, FL.

ROB WILLIAMS is a retired psychologist, the father of three, and the grandfather of four. He is also an avid golfer and bridge player. This excerpt is from his diary of a recent cross-country trip in a camper with his dog, Skeeter.